Love and Anger

Love
and
Anger

The Parental Dilemma

Nancy Samalin

with Catherine Whitney

Viking

VIKING
Published by the Penguin Group
Viking Penguin, a division of Penguin Books USA Inc.,
375 Hudson Street, New York, New York 10014, U.S.A.
Penguin Books Ltd, 27 Wrights Lane,
London W8 5TZ, England
Penguin Books Australia Ltd, Ringwood,
Victoria, Australia
Penguin Books Canada Ltd, 2801 John Street,
Markham, Ontario, Canada L3R 1B4
Penguin Books (N.Z.) Ltd, 182–190 Wairau Road,
Auckland 10, New Zealand

Penguin Books Ltd, Registered Offices:
Harmondsworth, Middlesex, England

First published in 1991 by Viking Penguin,
a division of Penguin Books USA Inc.

10 9 8 7 6 5 4 3 2 1

Portions of this book first appeared in
Health Magazine and Redbook.

Grateful acknowledgment is made for permission to reprint
"Some Things Don't Make Any Sense at All" from If I Were
in Charge of the World and Other Worries by Judith Viorst.
Reprinted with permission of Atheneum Publishers, an imprint of
Macmillan Publishing Company. Copyright © 1981 by Judith Viorst.

LIBRARY OF CONGRESS CATALOGING IN PUBLICATION DATA
Samalin, Nancy.
Love and anger : the parental dilemma / by Nancy Samalin
with Catherine Whitney.
p.   cm.
Includes bibliographical references.
Includes index.
ISBN 0–670–83136–0
1. Parenting. 2. Anger. 3. Discipline of children. 4. Love.
I. Whitney, Catherine. II. Title.
HQ755.8.S26   1991
649'.64—dc20   90–50602

Printed in the United States of America
Set in Goudy Old Style
Designed by Ann Gold

To Sy,
my constant source of love
and encouragement,
and to Tom,
with love, hope, and laughter

Acknowledgments

I am deeply grateful to the many hundreds of parents who shared their stories, thoughts, and insights with me during the writing of this book. It takes great courage to speak openly about such a difficult and complex subject, and I hope they know that their honesty and openness will help many others like themselves.

My sincere thanks to my editor, Nan Graham, whose belief in me and great instincts have been an inspiration for both my books. Likewise, the intelligence, attention to detail, and dedication of my literary agent, Jane Dystel, gave life and shape to this book from the beginning. I also appreciate the efforts of Marcia Burch and Janet Kraybill, at Penguin, for their help with my first book, *Loving Your Child Is Not Enough*.

Catherine Whitney, my collaborator, has made this project a pleasure. She has added a valuable perspective to a complicated topic, and it has been a privilege to work with her. No author could wish for a more receptive, responsible, efficient co-writer.

I am also grateful to Janet Schuler, who offered invaluable assistance in organizing the survey responses, transcribing tapes, and sorting through the substantial background material used for this book.

Many professionals have shared valuable information with me on the topic of anger and preventive mental health, including Dr. Rhoda Baruch and her capable staff at the Institute of Mental Health Initiatives; Dr. John Livingston, professor of psychiatry at Harvard Medical School; and Linda Braun and her colleagues at the Center for Parenting Studies of Wheelock College.

A special thanks is in order to those people who continue to help me reach parents and professionals in my community. In particular, my appreciation goes to Dr. Allen Collins, director of the department of psychiatry at Lenox Hill Hospital, who has enabled me to present the "How to Discipline with Love" programs, as well as to Dr. Susan Ginsberg, who for so long has supported my work at Bank Street College of Education.

Many colleagues and friends who have helped me in countless ways include Vicki Lansky, author of many books for parents and children; Gail Reichlin, director of the Parents Resource Network; Mary Solow, head of Central Synagogue Nursery School; as well as Arlette Brauer, Jean Soichet, Ruth Hersh, Molly Haskell, and Stefania Mc-Clennen. In addition, my associates, Robin Neiman and Ann Obsatz, deserve a special note of appreciation.

My sons, Eric and Todd, have taught me a great deal about being a parent. Besides being fine young adults with excellent values, they are a pleasure to have around. Their input is always honest, frequently funny, and usually on-target. A word of gratitude as well to my sister, Ellen Zanetti, and my brother, Tom Hettleman, who are always there for me when I need them. My stepmother, Ruth Hettleman, has been consistently generous, and I appreciate her pride in my work. And, as always, a special thanks to my mother, Elizabeth Kaufmann, whom I love and admire for her courage and zest for living.

Contents

Introduction

I became more and more resentful of her seeming rudeness and expressed my frustration by becoming critical. I criticized Ginger's table manners, the mess in which she left her room each morning, the way she threw her wet towel and dripping wash cloth on top of her soiled clothes, her extravagance in shopping at the most expensive stores, the loudness of her radio, and her refusal to wear her tooth-straightening apparatus. . . . I was obsessed with trying to make her behave.

I t may surprise you to learn that the author of the above was none other than Benjamin Spock, M.D., the man to whom millions of parents have turned for advice for more than forty years. His words refer to the parental crisis that occurred thirteen years ago when he became the stepfather of an eleven-year-old girl. In that situation, Dr. Spock reminds us, he was like any other parent—struggling to see through his anger to find a loving resolution.

I use this example to demonstrate that there are no absolute answers in this business of parenting. There are only the guidelines forged from our own experiences and the experiences of others. I am all too aware that I have learned the most important lessons over the years (as well as the most effective techniques) not only from my mentor, Dr. Alice Ginott, but also from the thousands of parents who have attended my lectures and workshops. In addition, many parents have written to me in response to my first book, *Loving Your Child Is Not Enough*, and have told me of their struggles to use effective discipline techniques— with the attendant successes and failures.

This caveat—that no single expert has all the answers— is important to note, for you will not find a series of no-fail solutions in the pages of this book. The subject of parents and anger is one that is by its very nature fraught with complexity. It is not my goal to provide a comprehensive overview of every manifestation of anger. And I leave it to the psychiatrists to probe the deep roots of anger as human expression. Rather, my goal here is to open a window on what is often considered to be a forbidden subject—to provide insights into the common issues that trigger anger between parents and their children, and to offer practical, positive ways to redirect that anger.

Most of all, it is my hope that parents who read this book will learn to judge themselves less harshly as they begin to see that many of their expressions of anger are completely normal. By their nature, children bring to the family environment disorder, aggravation, ambiguity, and turmoil. They also bring warmth, humor, boundless energy, and creativity. Loving parents wonder how they can encourage the latter while enduring the former. That dilemma is what we will explore in this book.

Love and Anger

1

The Parental Dilemma

I was the perfect father until my son was born.

—the parent of a two-year-old

Sharon stormed into the living room and kicked a stray toy with her foot. Her eyes flashed with fury as she glared at her son, Todd, who was happily immersed in the mess. "Damn it!" she screamed. "Why does this house always look like a disaster area?" She didn't wait for an answer, but flung her briefcase onto a chair and dumped her coat on top of it. "This is all I need after the day I've had. What's wrong with you anyway?"

Often, in a more lighthearted mood, Sharon had referred to seven-year-old Todd as the United House Wrecker. She could vividly describe how, within ten minutes of entering a room, her otherwise endearing son could easily turn everything in sight upside down, scattering socks, shirts, GI Joe dolls, blocks, crayons, toy cars, and broken pieces of cookie everywhere. She might not have minded so much if Todd had kept his messes confined to his room, but he was an equal-opportunity messer upper, and the living room was the most frequent target.

On this day, Sharon was in no mood to deal with Todd's

messes. She had had an awful time at work. She had lost a big account, and her boss had spent an hour telling her all the things she had done wrong. To make matters worse, she'd had to take the bus home because her car was in the shop. The bus was crowded and hot, and Sharon desperately wanted to be home, where she could relax and unwind. But as the bus bumped and jolted down the potholed streets, Sharon's mind kept spinning in its grim bad-day focus. As she envisioned walking in the door, she realized with a sick feeling that Todd would probably have the place in a wreck. In fact, she was sure of it. She closed her eyes and allowed herself to feel self-pity. Here she was working long and hard hours, and all she had to look forward to at the end of the day was a house that looked as if it had been hit by a tornado. Even the baby-sitter seemed helpless against Todd's house-messing skills. Why couldn't he realize how miserable it made her to come home to a mess, and show some consideration?

By the time Sharon walked in the door, she had already built up such an anger that she started yelling before she could stop herself. Now she stood towering over the chaos in her living room, hands planted on her hips and face contorted in rage. Todd knew his mother well enough to know when it was not a time for argument. "I'll clean it up," he said, motioning to the toys on the carpet.

But Sharon wasn't having any of that. "Oh, right, when hell freezes over! All I want is a little order, and I have to look at this mess. No matter what I do, no matter what I say, it's always the same thing. I've had it. I've just had it." She stormed into the kitchen and returned a moment later with a huge plastic garbage bag. Todd was anxiously scurrying to pick up toys, and when he saw his mother starting to shove them into the garbage bag, he became really alarmed. "I'll clean it up, Mom. Don't do that. What are you doing?" he babbled, running in circles around her.

"Teaching you a lesson," Sharon replied tightly. She finished stuffing the bag and with an air of finality, tied the top. As he watched her head toward the garbage chute in the hallway of their apartment building, Todd realized that she was not bluffing. She was really planning to throw out his favorite toys. "No, Mom, no!" he screamed, hurrying after her. But Sharon's anger was by now like a runaway express train, and she paid no attention to Todd's pleas. She shoved the bag into the chute and slammed the door shut. They could hear the bag thump-crash-thumping down three flights to the basement bin. Todd, beside himself with grief, wailed, "I hate you! I hate you! I wish you were dead."

Sharon took his arm and jerked him back into the apartment. "Don't you dare talk to me that way," she said, giving him a shake. "It served you right. Now, go to your room. I don't even want to see you for the rest of the evening."

After Todd ran sobbing to his room, Sharon felt momentarily better, but her satisfaction was almost immediately replaced by feelings of guilt, horror, and regret over what she had done. She realized that her anger had gotten completely out of control, that she had punished Todd not only for messing up the living room, but also for every bad thing that had happened to her that day. What on earth was wrong with her?

Sharon related this episode to the sympathetic ears of twelve other men and women who were gathered in one of my workshops in New York City to talk about parental anger. Although Sharon felt terrible about her behavior, few in the room seemed shocked by her story. In fact, I saw many parents nodding in reluctant recognition.

"After my husband came home from work, I spent about two hours in the basement going through trash bags from all the other apartments until I found Todd's toys," Sharon said sheepishly. "I apologized to Todd for having gotten so upset, and vowed to myself that I would never again allow my anger to get the better of me." Everyone smiled, sensing the impossibility of such a promise.

Sitting at the front of the room, listening to Sharon's story, I considered how many hundreds—or even thousands—of times in the past fifteen years I had heard similar stories. The subject of anger almost always comes up when parents gather, and it's a subject that troubles them a great deal. They believe that good parents don't yell, much less shriek, loving parents don't seethe with resentment, mature adults never give in to uncontrolled rage. They look to me for ways to exorcise these uncomfortable feelings, hoping that I'll offer them a solution, like a magic elixir, so they won't feel angry with their children anymore.

Instead, I tell them that the opposite is often true—the greater our love, the greater too our capacity for feeling a full range of troubling emotions, including anger, resentment, and even rage. It is only natural that these strong emotions are sometimes expressed in our relationships with our children, for they are the people in whom we invest our greatest love, our most intense feelings, and our highest expectations.

But it is not enough to say that it is normal for parents to feel angry with their children—just as it is normal for children to feel furious with their parents. We also must look at what our anger is doing to us, the impact it is having on our children, and how to deal with those powerful emotions that children arouse in us. The question is: How can we express our natural feelings of anger without hurting our children or attacking their self-esteem? And, at the same time, how can we teach our children to express their own feelings of anger in ways that are helpful, not hurtful?

For many families, home is a battleground, filled with

constant bickering, shouting matches, and exhausting power struggles. Often, parents' complaints appear so frivolous they hardly seem worth the effort of doing battle over. Parents are amazed that they can go from relative calm to utter frustration in a few seconds. An uneaten egg or spilled juice at breakfast can turn a calm morning into a free-for-all. In spite of parents' best intentions, bedtime becomes wartime, meals end with children in tears and food barely touched, and car rides deteriorate into stress-filled shouting matches.

Other battles take on more gravity; they occur when children fail to live up to parents' most cherished values— when they do poorly in school, lie, steal, or defy authority.

Whatever its source, we often experience parental anger as a horrifying encounter with our worst selves. I never even knew I had a temper until I had children. It was very frightening that these children I loved so much, for whom I had sacrificed so much, could arouse such intense feelings of rage in me, their mother, whose primary responsibility was to nurture and protect them.

Often, our anger may be unrelated to the incident at hand; it may be triggered by exhaustion, impatience, or the frustration that comes when events seem to be out of our control. Even though parents often find it hard to understand or accept their anger, most of them could easily make a list of the things their children do that push their "anger buttons." Sometimes in my workshops, I ask people to list their most common anger triggers. They easily think of many, and call them out:

When they won't do what I say.
When they won't take no for an answer.
When they defy me.

When they "hang" their clothes on the floor, and won't
clean up their rooms.

When I see them making the same mistakes I made.

When they act like helpless babies.

When they don't do their homework.

When they whine or argue in "that voice."

When they tune me out or ignore me, and become "parent deaf."

When they embarrass me or throw tantrums in public.

When they won't take responsibility for their belongings.

When they won't share with their friends or siblings.

When they try to boss *me* around.

When they don't show appreciation for the things I do
for them.

When they fight and bicker with one another.

When they give me that "attitude."

When they talk back and say things that hurt or insult
me.

When they say "I hate you" or "You're mean."

When they don't eat what I've prepared.

When they dawdle when I'm in a hurry.

When they won't go to or stay in bed.

And this is only a partial list. Usually, by the time people
have finished calling out their anger triggers, everyone is
laughing. There is something cathartic about the act of
sharing and the discovery that the reasons they get angry
are often very similar and leave other parents feeling just
as helpless. They are perplexed at the degree of anger they
feel over trivia. Parents often say "These reasons sound so
silly." Indeed, any parent who has ever wondered how a
child's refusal to eat his beans can generate a rage will agree
that the response often seems wildly out of proportion to
the "crime." They're ashamed of themselves, but I assure

them that anger is normal and even inevitable. It is my goal to help people realize that even the most loving, caring parents see red sometimes, and to reach an understanding of the many ways that anger is triggered—how it makes them feel and react the first time a child says "You're not the boss over me" or "I hate you," or when the child for whom they have such high hopes receives a C rather than an A in English. All parents experience these moments when they feel powerless to direct their children's lives—times when they doubt their ability to be effective and loving nurturers.

Fearing the Anger Monster

Anger doesn't discriminate between loving parents and negligent parents. This is a hard lesson for many people. Ted was a good example. One of the few men who attended my morning workshop, Ted was deeply committed to being a good father to his four-year-old daughter, Jessica. During the course of the workshops, Ted revealed that the reason he took parenting so seriously was that he wanted to avoid at all costs making the same mistakes his parents had made. Ted grew up in a tense and punitive home, where there were frequent angry confrontations between him and his parents. He remembered that as a child he had often felt intense feelings of hatred for his father, and he couldn't bear the idea that his daughter would ever have such feelings toward him. He bent over backward to avoid confrontations in their home, and described how he would always explain his restrictions carefully to his daughter so she would "understand" the reasons for his limits. "She knows why she has to be in bed by eight o'clock," Ted said. "And she can accept it because it doesn't just seem like an empty rule."

I could see how much Ted valued the solid communi-

cation that existed between him and his daughter, and I
didn't want to say anything that might burst his bubble.
But if there was one thing I knew about four-year-olds, it
was that they have a tremendous capacity for unreasonable
behavior, even given the most patient explanations. Although Ted and his daughter were close, by their very
nature preschoolers do not take kindly to the limits adults
set, no matter how reasonable and necessary these limits are.

One morning Ted arrived at the workshop, looking frazzled and distressed. "Tough morning, Ted?" I asked casually, when I noticed him staring glumly out the window.
He shrugged. "Not really . . . Jessica and I had a little
trouble at the playground this morning."

"Oh." I nodded. "Why don't you tell us about it—if you
want to."

Ted began describing the incident which had occurred
that morning on the playground at Jessica's nursery school.
When the weather was nice, he explained, he always tried
to arrive early so his daughter would have time to play in
the yard before school. Jessica really loved to climb on the
monkey bars, and Ted felt that this time they spent together
was very special. But that morning, when it was time to
stop playing and go inside, Jessica refused to come down
off the monkey bars. She defiantly told her father she didn't
want to go into the school; she wanted to stay outside and
play. As was his style, Ted tried to reason with his daughter,
gently reminding her that she had to come down now. It
was time for school to start. Daddy had to go. "Come on,
be a good girl," he said. But still she refused to come down.
He asked her a couple more times, and she ignored him
and continued to climb on the bars.

"By this time I was starting to get angry," Ted said guilt-
ily. "I was going to be late for this class, and she was going

to be late for school. She was being so unreasonable. Finally, I yelled 'Now!' and reached up and yanked her off the bars—at which point she started screaming at the top of her lungs, 'You're hurting me! You're hurting me!'

"I was shocked. She had rarely acted this oppositional with me before. I could see the other parents looking at me, wondering what I'd done. I was embarrassed. I felt like calling out 'I didn't hurt her.' She was crying and looking at me like I was the most rotten person in the world. She yelled, 'You're mean!' and ran into the school. Now, I really feel horrible." He shook his head in self-disgust. "I've ruined my daughter's day so I wouldn't be late for a class about how to be a better parent. What a joke! I should have let her play for a couple more minutes. I really blew it."

There is nothing unusual about Ted's story; it's the kind of mundane battle that happens all the time between parents and children when they have a conflict of needs. But it was a significant event for Ted because it showed him that conflicts between parents and children could not always be reasoned away. Of course, Jessica knew it was time to stop playing on the monkey bars. Of course, she realized that her father had to leave and that she was supposed to go into the school. She simply chose to ignore all of this information because she wanted to continue doing what was fun and didn't want to be stopped. Being four, she didn't care about the reasons. They were completely irrelevant to her. So when Ted insisted, she let him have it. "You're mean" or "You can't make me" is a heart stopper the first time a parent hears it.

Small as the incident might seem, it was nevertheless a big, day-ruining event for Ted. Ted needed to be firm without being punitive, but he also needed to accept the inevitable—that Jessica would be upset at having to stop what she was doing and accede to his wishes. Perhaps he could have given Jessica a choice instead of an order, saying "Jessica, you'd like to stay and play, but we're going in now. You can walk, or I'll carry you." And even if she continued to whine or cry, he needed to carry her in and be prepared for her being temporarily upset and mad at him.

In some households, these minor battles are strung together until it seems that the only interactions are confrontations. Parents whose children say accusingly "You're *always* yelling at me" are startled by the realization that their children don't view them as the benevolent, loving people they believe themselves to be. They wonder, "Is this the way my child sees me—as someone who is always yelling?" As one parent in the workshop observed, "To the outside world, I'm thought of as a gentle, kind, patient person. If only they could see me with my kid."

The Inevitable Emotion

"Was this normal? I wondered. Was my anger normal?" So asked C. W. Smith, a divorced father, in his book *Uncle Dad*—an honest portrayal of a weekend dad's struggle with love and anger. "They could make me furious," he wrote. "Their behavior was dreadful. In the supermarket I'd set Keith in the cart; his bright little eyes would scan the colorful shelves and his arms would reach out for things. He'd wail if he didn't get them. Or he would want to get out of the cart so he could walk by himself. If I insisted that he hold my hand, he'd go limp in the aisle. To anyone who has never experienced a howling sit-down strike by a two- or three-year-old in a crowded supermarket, I say you've never known real humiliation. You understand how Gandhi won India. . . ."

Is there a parent alive who cannot empathize with what Smith was experiencing in that supermarket aisle? Every parent knows how it feels, and it's something you never forget. In supermarkets, you will say things to your children that you wouldn't say to your worst enemy, things your parents said to you that you vowed never to say when you became a parent. When I read Smith's description, I noticed that, even though I was many years past the agony of a toddler-on-strike in the supermarket aisle (my sons are grown men now), I remembered the excruciating embarrassment of my son's hysterical tantrums on the Broadway bus almost every day—after he'd spent three hours in nursery school keeping his emotions in check. It felt as if he'd been saving up all the hysteria for me!

Out in the world, parents are all too aware of the eyes of strangers watching them. One mother told the story of the day she took her two-year-old to the bank. The child was cranky, whining as she sat in her stroller, and the mother felt tense because the line was long. Suddenly, a fly started buzzing around the child's head, and angrily the child flicked it away and said very loudly, "Fucking fly!" The mother felt her face redden as all conversation in the line stopped. She could just imagine what people were thinking. Her first impulse was to slap the child. But instead she went with her second impulse. She looked at her son and said in a very loud voice, "Wait until I tell your mother what you just said!"

People laugh when I relate this story, because most parents identify with the poor, embarrassed mother. I tell parents in my workshops that when they are the recipients of public humiliation inflicted by their irrational toddlers or preschoolers, and they are being stared at by clucking strangers, to repeat this mantra: "I do not know these people. They are not my friends. I will never see them again."

No one was more surprised than I the first time I heard myself screaming out of control at one of my children. I had always considered myself a very mild person. No one had ever accused me of having a temper, and, in fact, when I was a teacher (before my own children were born), parents sometimes remarked on what they considered to be my endless reserves of patience. Then, suddenly, with the arrival of my sons, born only twelve months apart, there emerged this snarling Other Me. Like nearly all the parents I have met over the years, I was myself an early victim of the mundane parent/child battles. I nagged, criticized, threatened, and argued with my two sons more often than I like to admit. And I was troubled by how frequently my reaction to petty incidents was one of sudden anger.

Everyone gets angry. But when it comes to parental anger, many people find it hard to accept that such an intensity of negative feelings could be radiating from them to their (normally) beloved, innocent children.

If our capacity to feel terrible anger for the children we love distresses us, it is our capacity to speak and act from those angry feelings that so often fills us with horror and self-loathing. As Dr. Haim Ginott, the noted child psychologist, once wrote:

> The English language has a rich supply of expressions to give vent to all nuances of anger. . . . Anger colors our vision. We turn white with anger, and purple with rage. We see red. We cannot see straight. We go blind. We are livid. . . . Our eyes spit fire. . . . We fume, we smolder, we sizzle, we stew, we flare up, we boil over, we explode, we blow our stack, blow our top, fly off the handle, hit the ceiling, raise the roof.

A mother once told me that she happened to catch sight of herself in a mirror while she was screaming at her son in a state of uncontrolled rage. What she saw shocked her.

"It was this wild-looking woman with a contorted face, and I thought, My God, that's me!"

Uncontrolled rage is scary. It's like being possessed by a demon. When we are in this state, we may want to inflict pain or take revenge on the person who is making our lives so miserable. Horace described anger as "a short madness," and this state of rage feels exactly like madness. When we scream "I'm going to kill you" or "This will teach you" or "Now you're going to be sorry," that is exactly the way we feel at that moment—and these age-old expressions are all statements of revenge and vindictiveness.

The trigger for rage can be something as mundane as a child who doesn't answer when we've called her for the third time. Or it can be a teenager defying us when we lay down rules. Maybe it's a combination of factors, including being overtired, that lead to the explosion.

Many parents have expressed guilt and fear about their rages, wondering if they are potential abusers. Their feeling is so intense, it frightens them. Barbara described how she felt when her ten-year-old daughter defied her and went next door to visit a friend after Barbara had told her she wasn't to leave the house. In a fury, Barbara picked up the phone and called her daughter. "Come home this minute or don't bother to come home at all," she shouted. Later, when she had calmed down, she felt terrible about having said those words. "What could I have been thinking to say 'don't come home at all'?" she wondered. "It was a very cruel thing to say. Jennifer's a sensitive child. What if she had taken me seriously and gone wandering out on the street? What kind of a parent would ever speak like that to her child?"

When we don't know alternative responses for our anger, we automatically say and do things that we regret. In the instant of our rage, we *want* to hurt the person who is causing us so much trouble—to get even in some way. We say and do things we don't mean (or wouldn't mean in a more temperate mood), and once we've calmed down, we wish we could take them back.

When Anger Hurts

Nan, the parent of a three-year-old boy, Jay, described in one of my classes how she lost control of her temper. Although she was able to turn the situation around once she had regained her composure, Nan regretted her explosion. She described the scene this way:

It was Sunday morning, and she decided to surprise Jay with a special breakfast.

JAY (angry): I don't want Apple Jacks. I want Alphabits.
NAN: Why don't you have Alphabits tomorrow?
JAY: No! [He throws the bowl on the floor, milk and all.]
NAN (slapping him furiously): Get out of my sight! I'm so angry with you.

After several minutes, Nan wasn't feeling so angry anymore. She felt bad about hitting Jay, and went into his room, where he was sitting on his bed crying.

NAN: I don't like hitting you. I'm sorry. I just lost my temper and went crazy.
JAY: Next time I'll hit you back.
NAN: Let's not hit at all when we get angry. Let's just count to ten so we won't hit or throw things. Mommies get real angry sometimes, and so do little boys.
JAY: You know why I did it. I said I wanted Alphabits.
NAN: From now on, I won't surprise you. You can pick out what you want for breakfast.

JAY: That's a good idea.
NAN (handing him a sponge): Why don't you go clean up the mess and then you can pick out your cereal.
JAY (cheerfully): Okay.

When Jay defied her by throwing his cereal on the floor, Nan felt blinded by her anger. She could think of nothing to do but strike back at him—get even with him for his being so naughty. There are a number of things she could have done instead of hitting Jay. For example, given the heat of her anger, it would have been better if she had left the room until she calmed down. She might have said very firmly, "Jay, I am so angry with you right now, I will not stay in the same room with you," and walked out of the kitchen, allowing both of them a few minutes to calm down.

People often confuse feeling with doing. Their automatic impulse goes "I feel angry, therefore I scream [or hit]." For this reason, they are just as guilty about their angry feelings as they are about their angry actions. For example, a parent who wishes fervently, in the heat of emotion, that she'd never had children might later be overcome with guilt that she could even *think* such a horrible thing. But thinking and feeling aren't the same as saying and doing, and we have to learn to separate our feelings from the way we act. Sometimes when we give ourselves permission to feel our anger, it can serve as a release. One mother told me of an incident that occurred at the A&P. Her young daughter was screaming hysterically in a high-pitched voice, and she wouldn't stop. The mother experienced a brief fantasy, in which she set the child down on the checkout counter and asked if anyone would like to adopt her. The fantasy made her smile, and suddenly she didn't feel so angry anymore.

Another mother once described her rage when her nine-year-old son refused to go to bed. "I was so mad, I felt like dismembering him!"

I smiled and replied, "Yes, but you didn't."

Our goal, then, is not to eliminate the *feelings* of anger from our parental repertoire. We couldn't, even if we wanted to. Rather, it is to find ways to express ourselves when we are angry that do not hurt, insult, demean, or inspire revenge and rage in our children.

When we examine the most common ways parents verbally express anger, the words are often designed to wound:

We use accusing, blaming, or defensive language.
You're disgusting—a slob!
It's all your fault.
How can you be so stupid?
You're just a spoiled brat!

We overgeneralize or catastrophize.
I'll never be able to trust you again.
You're always screwing up.
You're grounded for the rest of your life.
I can never count on you.
You'll never amount to anything.

We lecture or preach.
I want to get one thing straight with you . . . I expect you to [blah-blah-blah] . . . and from now on you had better listen to me when I say [blah-blah-blah] . . . it's about time you realized [blah-blah-blah] . . . I'm only looking out for your own [blah-blah-blah]. . . . When I was a child, I never [blah-blah-blah-blah, and so on].

We issue commands and threats.
Get over here this minute.

If you don't apologize this second, you'll be in big trouble.
If you do that one more time, you're dead.
Wait until I tell your father what you did!

These are just a few of the most common ways we issue verbal put-downs when we are angry with our children. The other thing we do, of course, is punish them. However, most of the time our punishments fail because we want to teach our child a lesson but we are not providing a situation conducive to learning. Punishment often causes the child to be filled with rage and the desire to get even. There's a story that psychologist David Elkind tells about a punishment that backfires. In the story, a little girl was acting obnoxious, whining, and pushing all her mother's buttons. The mother was on a short fuse that day, feeling very tired and vulnerable to her daughter's provocative behavior. So she said to her, "You'd better stop it." And her daughter imitated her, saying "Nyaa, nyaa, nyaa," followed by "You're stupid" or "You're doody" or something equally unacceptable. By now the mother was completely enraged. So she did the first thing that came to her mind. She shut her daughter in the closet. (It was mother's closet, since this scene occurred in her bedroom.) And, after five minutes, the mother started to feel guilty, so she stood outside the closet door, about to open it. But it was very quiet inside, so she said to her daughter through the door, "What are you doing in there?" And her daughter retorted, "I'm spitting on your shoes and I'm spitting on your clothes." The mother was quite taken aback, because she had hoped her daughter was sitting in the closet feeling remorseful about her rude behavior. She opened the door, and her daughter didn't come out, and she said impatiently, "Now what are you doing?" And her daughter replied, "I'm waiting for more spit."

The problem with the knee-jerk reactions that come from rage is that the punishment is usually not one we would choose in a more rational moment. And although our intention is that the punishment will inspire contrition in our children, it often leads to feelings of revenge instead. No lesson is learned, and parent and child alike feel angry and frustrated.

Probably, had the mother in this story given herself a cool-down period, she would not have shut her daughter in the closet as a punishment. It was an action taken in the heat of anger, and those actions are almost always ineffective or, worse, hurtful. So, the goal is to learn how to feel anger fully, to acknowledge its legitimacy as a human emotion, but to avoid acting from that point of angry irrationality. It's often possible to do this, with the help of the skills which we'll discuss in this book.

Sharing Our Struggle with Anger

As I was preparing to write this book, I developed a survey, which I handed out to parents who attended my lectures and workshops. I believe that one of the most valuable ways we can help one another is by sharing our ideas and experiences. I have seen the way parents can benefit from being in groups, and I thought the survey would be another way to enable them to put the issue of anger into perspective. When they hear many other voices articulating feelings that they have had (and been ashamed of or worried about), it can help them see their experiences in a different way.

Nearly one hundred parents supplied their input through the surveys. (See Appendix B for a list of the survey questions.) The parents who responded represent a variety of backgrounds and experiences. In total, they have 186 children:

> 98 boys
> 88 girls
> _____
> 70 infants, toddlers, preschoolers
> 90 elementary school children
> 26 junior high, high school children

Throughout the book, I will occasionally highlight the relevant responses I received from survey participants. The authenticity of their observations, as well as the observations of those in my workshops, add weight to the discussion of parental anger. It is my hope that this book will open up a fresh dialogue and, perhaps for the first time, bring the issue of parental anger out of the closet so that we can acknowledge it and find ways to resolve the critical dilemma we face between our love and our anger.

2

Everyday Madness

My ability to parent is directly proportionate to the amount
of sleep I've gotten.   —a mother in my workshop

Kevin, a young father who attended one of my workshops, jotted down a poignant recollection from his
own childhood, part of which he read to the group
one day:

MOM: Look at your room! It is a complete disaster area. I
want you to pick up all your clothes, make your bed,
and *how many times* do I have to tell you not to bring
dishes in here. It's no wonder we never have any glasses
to drink out of. Hurry up and do it now, because if you
miss the bus and I have to drive you to school again, I
swear I will not buy you that hockey stick you want so
much.

KEVIN: But . . . Mom . . .

MOM: Just do as I say!

"At the mention of the hockey stick, I went into a state
of panic. I quickly gathered my things around the room,

and tried to make a semblance of order that my mother would accept. At age thirteen, I really wanted my own hockey stick, instead of having to use the ones at school, which were always too big or too small. I was determined not to miss the bus, and fled out the front door, only to hear my mother scream 'Kevin, did you brush your teeth?' I pretended not to hear her, and sprinted up the steps of the bus. I made it! My anger diminished as I thought of which hockey stick I would be purchasing later that day."

When Kevin had finished reading, he sat for a moment staring down at his paper. "It's funny," he said finally. "I can still remember this incident as if it were yesterday. I used to really resent my mother's insistence that my room be clean every morning. It didn't make any sense to me. No one would see it during the day, and if she didn't go upstairs, she wouldn't see it either. I thought there must be more important things in life than keeping a clean room."

I smiled at Kevin. His story was a good example of the ordinary parent-child struggles that take place in most households. His mother wanted a clean room, but it was the last thing on Kevin's mind. He considered it unimportant, but it was something that really made her mad. I turned to the class. "How many of you get angry with your children over what you consider trivial matters—like a messy room, or an unfinished dinner, or a refusal to bathe or go to bed on time?" The response was predictable—many nods of the head and several sheepish smiles.

"And how many of you feel guilty about that because you believe anger should be reserved for the really important issues?" I asked. More nods of the head.

"Well, shouldn't it be?" asked Michele, a bit impatiently. "I don't exactly feel like a model of parenthood when I lose my temper over a silly thing like my daughter, Marissa, nagging me in the store to buy her an overpriced doll she desperately wants. I feel like a shrew."

"You're concerned about how little things can cause so much anger in you." I nodded. "Most parents are."

"What amazes me is that even though I can remember so clearly my resentment over my mother's harping, I don't act any differently with my own son," Kevin admitted. "For me, it's his terrible dawdling. It drives me crazy."

Whining and nagging. Dawdling. Messy rooms. Fighting with siblings. Refusing to go to bed. These are typical anger triggers for parents. In my workshops, we often spend the bulk of our time talking about conflicts that arise from daily nitty-gritty situations. Parents often confess that they feel silly talking about mundane events like a child who refuses to go to bed without fussing, or the one who nags for a toy at the store. They feel that only "real" problems should be worth losing one's temper about. But if your home is a daily battleground, you know there's nothing trivial about these complaints. The incidents add up and make you feel frustrated, guilty, and out of control.

Parents who responded to my survey were in accord on the subject of everyday anger triggers. Here are just a few of the occasions for anger they noted:

When I have to ask my daughter ten times before she starts setting the table.

Whining. Especially when I'm trying to make dinner.

I get most angry when my toddler dawdles—which she always does when I'm in a hurry.

That nonstop grating voice—"Mama, Mama, Mama . . ."

If I don't nag them or bribe them with dessert, I can't get them to eat their main course.

My son takes forever to wake up in the morning, and then he drags his feet getting ready for school. We usually have a fight about his not eating breakfast, and I end up yelling.

At the end of a long day when my children are exhausted, and so am I, and they won't go to bed. This makes me very angry!

When he won't eat after I've spent an hour preparing his dinner.

When she changes her mind five times about which pants to wear to school that day—and the bus is due any minute.

When my son constantly interrupts me while I'm on the phone, until finally I am forced to hang up.

In my workshops, I try to help parents feel less guilty about getting mad, which is very natural, while at the same time offering them techniques that can alleviate the everyday anger they talk about. I asked Michele, the self-proclaimed "shrew," to talk more about what happened when her daughter wanted something in the store.

"Marissa is six, and she has a dreadful case of the gimmes," said Michele. "Her nagging drives me crazy. You say no and no and no, and it's exhausting. As soon as we enter a store, she starts begging me for a toy, a book, a Barbie outfit, candy. It embarrasses me that my daughter is so greedy. She's a bottomless pit of wants, and she won't be satisfied until she has everything that was ever manufactured by mankind—and then some."

"What do you say to her when she begins her begging litany?" I asked Michele.

"I tell her she has more than enough toys, and that she's never satisfied no matter how much I buy for her."

I suggested, "What if you said instead, 'I can see how much you like that doll, but I'm not ready to buy it for you right now.' Of course, you'll get a hundred buts. Kids have plenty of time to try to persuade you to get them what they want. They're not so busy! But they have the right to ask, and you have the right to refuse. Another way to handle it is to say 'I'm not ready to buy that today, but why don't you put it on your wish list.' "

"What do I say when she asks 'Why can't you?' "

"Just because a child asks for a reason, doesn't mean you have to supply it. It will only lead to more arguing, because the child will always try to persuade you to change your mind. It's a no-win situation."

Michele frowned. "No matter how I say it, she's still going to be upset."

"Of course she is!" I smiled. "Don't expect your daughter to react with equanimity and say 'I understand, Mother dear. It's okay.' "

More likely, children will be angry, because when people don't get what they want, it often makes them mad. Give a child permission to be mad, sad, or disappointed, and try not to be too critical of her wanting. Michele could also say to herself, "Marissa is entitled to want it, and I'm entitled to say no." I like that, because it communicates that she's an okay person for wanting things. Many of us were brought up to feel that we were greedy or selfish if we wanted things. Our parents turned our wants into occasions for shame. Even as adults, we are sometimes embarrassed to admit that we care about having more money, or that we envy our neighbor's fancy car or designer clothes. Marissa is not a bad, greedy, ungrateful child because she wants what catches her eye in the store. Michele's job as a parent, however, is often to say no to these seemingly endless desires.

My point is, we are not as helpless as we might think to change these situations. Having skills in the way we respond can make a difference and make us feel less at the mercy of our impulses. Most parents think they should be able to handle the everyday stuff automatically, but why should they think that, since no one ever taught them how? On the contrary, I imagine that most of us were raised in households where the dynamics were very similar to the ones described here, in which we were told repeatedly that the things we wanted were not worth making a fuss over. When I was little, if I said "I'm scared of the dark," my parents would say "There's nothing to be scared of. Go back to bed, you're just stalling." Or, if I wanted a special doll, and I begged my mother for it, she would give me a speech about how I had three dolls at home and I didn't need another one, and remind me of how fortunate I was compared to all the poor little girls all over the world who didn't have dolls. And when she finished telling me why I shouldn't want what I wanted, I still wanted it just as badly—only I felt ashamed of myself for wanting it.

When we acknowledge our children's right to want things, as well as their right to be upset when they can't have what they want, it can go a long way toward defusing their anger and the tantrums that occur as a result.

Edward, a father who came to one of my workshops, told the story of being on a public bus with his daughter, Teri. As soon as they boarded the bus, Teri began to wail—crying hysterically, body shaking. Of course, everyone was staring, so Edward felt as though he were onstage. He admitted that his first reaction was to "shake the living daylights" out of his child. Instead, he put his arms around Teri.

EDWARD: Teri, you are so upset. What's wrong?

TERI (sobbing): I left my wand at Kelly's house.

EDWARD: You really feel bad about leaving it at her house.

TERI: Wah, wah! I want to get it.

EDWARD: You want to go back and get it, but we can't stop now. The bus is crossing Central Park. [Here, Edward was trying to reason with her, which usually doesn't work too well.]

TERI: I want it now. Please, Daddy! [Big sobs.]

EDWARD (hugging her): I know, I know.

Eventually, Teri quieted down, and Edward reported proudly that a woman on the bus said to him, with admiration, "I don't know how you did it. You did everything just right." Edward agreed. "I thought I did a pretty good job too. In the past, I would have gotten mad and tried to shut her up, because I was worried about appeasing the people on the bus, not Teri."

If Edward had responded with anger at his daughter's bus drama, there is little doubt that Teri's hysteria would have escalated. By allowing her the right to feel bad about leaving her wand behind, which was very important to her, and by being empathetic instead of treating Teri as though her concerns were trivial, Edward helped gain her cooperation and calmed her by his nonjudgmental response to what seemed to *him* to be much ado about nothing.

The Anger Reflex

I sometimes ask parents in my workshops to perform an exercise that is, I admit, somewhat masochistic: Leave a tape recorder on during breakfast or dinner, to record what you say and how you say it. When my children were younger, I tried it, and I got a terrible shock. I often tell parents about this watershed experience: the discovery that instead of being a gracious, peace-loving person, I would have made an excellent Marine drill sergeant: *Sit up straight . . . button your shirt . . . leave me alone . . . stop touching your brother . . . finish your toast . . . how many times do I have to tell you to stop rocking the chair . . . close the refrigerator . . . keep your hands to yourself . . . be quiet . . . listen when I talk to you . . . what's the matter with you?*—this was the way I talked. It came naturally. I was embarrassed to hear myself on tape, and I felt discouraged. Here we were, a family who loved one another, but to hear us around the breakfast table, you'd never guess it, since all that issued from my mouth were commands and judgments, delivered in a nagging, petulant, critical tone.

I agonized over this and wondered why I could not respond in a more loving or at least rational way. Not only did my raving seem to fall on deaf ears—it never produced the desired response—but it made both me and my children miserable. I feared that I was damaging my children's self-esteem with my harsh words, and my fear was well-founded. Unchecked expressions of anger often lead to our making negative statements that communicate to our children that we think they are unlovable. Think about the common expressions we use that sound blaming when we fly off the handle:

What's wrong with you?
Were you born in a barn?
You'll pay for this!
You will never learn.
You're a slob.

You're rotten.
You're driving me crazy.
You're being ridiculous.
You're a bad boy [or girl].
Are you deaf [blind, dumb]?
You don't have a brain in your head.
For once in your life, I wish you'd . . .
Can't you do anything right?
I've had it up to here with you.
You impossible brat!
Why don't you grow up?
You're going to be the death of me!

When our children listen to us, they often perceive our words as accusations or attacks. When we tell them what to do, they complain that we're always on their backs. Of course, we don't call it nagging or attacking. We call it *reminding,* as in *Did you remember your book report . . . your lunch . . . your gym shorts? Don't forget your bus pass. Don't forget to comb your hair . . . brush your teeth . . . hang up your dress,* and so on. We reason that, once they start behaving as they should, we will stop reminding. As one mother said to me, "I won't nag at Joey to pick his clothes up off the floor when he starts picking his clothes up off the floor."

When, after these well-meaning reminders, our children fail to respond or continue to be forgetful anyway, we're angry: "I reminded you! How could you forget? Are you deaf? Stupid? Trying to drive me crazy?" But often after we have vented our disgust and anger, we may then rush to bail them out, so that they won't have to suffer or be unhappy for having been forgetful, irresponsible, or care-less. We want our children to be more responsible, but how often do we really give them a chance? We forget that the best way children learn is by experiencing the consequences of their actions. Using consequences as a substitute for fighting and nagging helps children cooperate. Penny, who had attended one of my lectures, later told me how she handled the chronic lateness of her nine-year-old son, Ken.

"He was always late getting out to the school bus. We would invariably have that last terrible ten minutes, filled with yelling, fighting, and crying. Half the time, he'd miss the bus, and I would end up driving him to school, feeling angry as hell.

"Then, as you suggested, I explained to Ken that it was time for him to take on the responsibility of being ready to leave for the bus on time—that if he missed the bus, I would take him to school when I could, but it would not necessarily be right away. Ken really loves school and likes to get there early to play with his friends, so this meant something to him. One morning soon after this conversation, he missed the bus. I think maybe he was trying to test me—to see if I really meant to follow through or if it was just an idle threat. Without yelling, anger, or recriminations, I did my chores, which included walking the dog, washing the breakfast dishes, and straightening up the living room. Then I showered and dressed. At 9:45, I drove Ken to school and kissed him good-bye. He had to go to the office for a late pass. Since then he has gotten ready for the bus on time. Mornings have been much smoother, without so much yelling and crabbiness."

Another mother, Hilda, who remarked that her son, Gene, "would forget his head if it wasn't screwed on," described in my workshop how frustrated she was that he continued to be so forgetful and thoughtless.

"Last week was a good example. Gene forgot his lunch after I had reminded him several times that morning. He then called me from school, just as I was running out the door, already late for an appointment. I started to get angry when I first heard his voice on the phone. He said, 'Ma, I forgot my lunch. Will you bring it to me?' I was mad, but I felt I had to run to the school, and I missed my appointment, so I was pretty worked up by the time I arrived with Gene's lunch box. We stood in the hallway, and I said, 'Thanks to your forgetfulness, I've missed my appointment. I reminded you, and you paid no attention to me. And this is the last time. Next time you can just go hungry.' Instead of apologizing, he got mad and defensive, saying with a smart mouth 'I suppose *you* never forget anything—you're so perfect.' "

So, what do you say in response to the call "Please, Mom, pretty please, could you bring my lunch?" You might say "It just isn't possible for me today." Be gracious about it, don't blame, but be firm. Hilda bailed Gene out, but he was not grateful, nor did he learn what can happen when he forgets to bring something he needs to school.

Elise, the parent of an eight-year-old girl, Molly, shook her head. "I find that if I say I can't, it just makes her angry, and I feel like a terrible mother."

That's okay. Of course Molly's angry. Kids don't like it when parents don't do what they want. And it's hard for parents to hear "I hate you," "You're mean," "You don't care if I starve." But it's important to keep the focus. When parents come to the rescue, they may feel better initially, but letting children experience the consequences of their actions will ultimately be the more powerful teacher. The issue is not whether you love your child. The issue is how to allow children to experience the consequences of their actions while keeping the focus on the matter at hand. A mother I know found a way to handle the "You don't love me" accusation with great aplomb. She had started yelling when she saw her daughter about to walk in muddy boots

across her just-mopped floor. "Amanda, don't you *dare* walk
in here with those boots. Out!" Amanda started to cry,
saying "You don't love me." The mother didn't miss a beat.
She replied, "Right now we're not talking about love, we're
talking about muddy boots that belong outside."

Beating the Bad-Day Syndrome

Nearly everyone has at some time expressed what I call
"spillover anger." Willard Gaylin, M.D., describes it this
way in his book *The Rage Within:*

> Returning from a frustrating, humiliating day at work, a parent
> or spouse will find any excuse to explode at the safer but more
> vulnerable people around him rather than at the indifferent
> and threatening authority who generated the rage. An infrac-
> tion that would be ignored under normal circumstances pro-
> duces a sudden and violent outburst.

It is easy after a day full of hassles to experience a child
as being just one more hassle, one more person who wants
to sap our strength. We feel emotionally fragile and put
upon. We long to have someone take care of us and soothe
our emotions. Instead, we are required to take care of a
child who might be exhausted and needy as well, and who
is acting unreasonable. This child can become the enemy
in our battle to have a moment's peace. Things look very
different when we're tired. As one mother complained to
me, "I feel like I don't have the energy to be a parent."
This is a common refrain from parents who sometimes feel
so overwhelmed they can hardly take care of themselves,
much less their tired, rambunctious, demanding children.
Remember Sharon, who threw her son's toys down the
garbage chute? Her anger over his messiness was exacer-

bated by her having had a bad day. She had been mad at her boss, but she couldn't yell at him. She saved it up until she got home, and erupted then. Sharon wasn't a bad person for spilling out her day's rage in this way. But like many parents who find themselves experiencing an end-of-the-day pileup of anger, she sought an outlet that would be less destructive.

Brad, the father of two active little boys, described his frustration. "I love them," he told me, "but at the end of the day, sometimes the last thing I want to do is to walk into that house and be swept up in the turmoil. I'm okay on the weekends, when it's more relaxed, but during the week it's very hard not to be an ogre. My wife, Connie, is home with the kids, so she can't wait to see me walk in the door and take over. One day last week, I walked in to find my wife in tears in the kitchen, and the boys jumping on the couch in the living room. School had been closed that day because of snow, and they had been stuck in the house together for ten hours. My wife saw me and screamed, 'God, you're finally home. Now, *you* deal with them!' I started yelling about how hard I worked and how tired I was, and soon we were shouting back and forth. Suddenly, I turned around and saw Benjy, our three-year-old, standing in the doorway to the kitchen, watching us with a wide-eyed, solemn face. He said, 'Daddy, why are you mad at Mommy?' I realized how frightening we must have sounded to him. I felt terrible."

It was easy to empathize with this father who was torn between his desire to show love for his children and his need to have some time for himself. Most people are not at the top of their form after a hard day at work, yet often it's the only time they have available to spend with their children. I told Brad that it was understandable that he would need a break at the end of the day, after he took off his manager hat and before he put on his daddy hat. "If you don't take a break, you're going to be carrying all the baggage from your job into your evening. The reason you feel like a better parent on weekends is that you're more relaxed. What could you think of that might ease the transition from work to home?"

Brad reported his solution a few weeks later. "We have a den in the basement, and at the top of the stairs is the living room. The kids are running back and forth, up and down the stairs. They take over the whole house, so there's no place to find peace. Last week, after talking it over with my wife, I announced a new rule. I realized that not only did I need that quiet time before the evening began—we all needed a chance to wind down. The new rule was, when I walked in at six, everyone would get a big hug, just like always; then we would set the timer for twenty minutes, and that would be our family quiet time. The boys could do what they wanted—play quietly or read—but they weren't to interrupt Mommy and Daddy unless it was an emergency. So far, it has worked pretty well. When there are lapses, I remind them of the rule."

Brad's decision to create an oasis of peace for his family was a step in the direction of easing the tensions that are a part of everyday family life. Parents and children alike need space for themselves, and once he had reclaimed that space, Brad felt less angry and resentful of the demands of parenthood. Sometimes a little change can go a long way toward replacing chaos with cooperation. And parents who think that it would be impossible to establish such a policy might be surprised at how well it works when they do it with regularity. Children respond well to routines that are repeated every day.

Remember that children experience spillover anger too, and sometimes their seemingly unreasonable tantrums are the outpouring of an accumulation of incidents. Developmental psychologist Aletha J. Solter, Ph.D., calls this "the broken cookie syndrome." Solter writes in *Parent and Preschooler*, a newsletter for parents of young children,

> Sometimes the crying will seem reasonable to you, but at other times it will appear to be totally unjustified by the situation that triggered it. A cookie breaks and the child cries as if her whole world has fallen apart! This kind of crying and raging is just as important to accept as the kind that seems more reasonable, because children accumulate painful feelings and then release them all at once in intense crying sessions triggered by small events. Children do not usually verbalize the real issue they are crying about, but this is not necessary for the crying to be beneficial.

Kids Will Be Kids

When parents complain about a two-year-old throwing a tantrum, a ten-year-old failing for the hundredth time to take out the garbage, or a twelve-year-old tuning them out, they are often surprised when I remind them that their children's behavior is perfectly normal for their ages. It helps relieve some of the pressure when we remember that every child goes through similar stages. Elizabeth Crary, in her book *Pick Up Your Socks*, lists some standard behaviors parents report about their children at different ages. Common behavior for toddlers includes dawdling and saying no. Between three and six, children interrupt and whine. At seven and eight, there's daydreaming and failure to do chores. At nine and ten, it's teasing siblings, failing to do chores, and interrupting. Eleven- and twelve-year-olds talk back, and thirteen-year-olds have trouble getting up in the morning, ignore what parents say, and are often very moody.

This is behavior that we should expect. It's not necessarily acceptable, and I'm not suggesting that parents should go along with it simply because it normally occurs. However, it helps to recognize that a behavior pattern is normal. Often we are shocked when we see our children acting out the behavior that is typical of their ages. For instance, we might say to a five-year-old "What's wrong with you? You're always whining." Or to an eleven-year-old, "How many times do I have to tell you to take out the garbage? You only think of your own needs—you're so selfish!" Or to a thirteen-year-old, "I don't understand why your room has to look like a pigsty all the time." We often treat our children as though they are the first children in history to exhibit such terrible behavior. In our anger, we communicate to them that "good" children don't behave in those ways when in fact good children do. Instead of acknowledging that this is appropriate developmental behavior, we think our children are doing things deliberately to drive us crazy.

Many parents find the toddler stage especially difficult. I often use an anonymous poem to remind parents of toddlers that what they are experiencing is normal. It is called "What to Expect of Your Toddler."

He will reach into every closet,
every door, every cupboard in the house.

He will indiscriminately
taste, touch, chew, pull on, lick, jerk, bite,
and swallow every particle he can reach—
and he can reach them all.

He will not be afraid of water
even if it's 3000 feet deep.
He will not know the potentials of fire
even if it's 3000 degrees hot.
He will not be afraid of autos and tractors
even if they are 3000 pounds heavy.

He will resent
ignore
and crawl away from all your warnings
but wiggle into your heart.

Since the developmental stages bring with them predictable behavior, we need to know as much as possible
about what is developmentally appropriate so that we don't
overreact. Remember, children can neither be shamed nor
bullied into changing. In our logical adult minds, we sometimes think that if we can convince our children that they
are wrong, they will change for the better.

A woman in my group who was struggling with her children's childishness, saw the light herself when she began
to remember scenes from her own childhood. "My eighth-
grade teacher was very critical of me because I wasn't as
obedient in her class as my older brother had been. She
used to go on and on about how she couldn't understand
why I wasn't more like my brother. I know she believed
that, if she just said it enough times, it would finally sink
in, and I would change. But the opposite happened. I hated
her every time she mentioned Greg's name. And I hated
him, too. If anything, my behavior only grew worse. Now,
I realize I do the same thing with my daughter when I hold
up her sister as an example of the way she should be."

Problems are most effectively resolved when we state our
expectations clearly in advance. We can't expect children

to know the rules automatically. Two-year-olds don't know that it's not okay to put spaghetti up their noses unless we tell them. It's up to us to spell out guidelines briefly and firmly, preferably in a neutral manner, without criticizing the child. For example, "Seat belts must be worn in the car and put on before we start." Or "In this home, we use words; we don't hit." And if you realize that it is typical for four-year-olds to whine, and you can't stand whining, think about how you might create ground rules to help alleviate the whining. One parent told me of her solution, which worked fairly well. She told her son, "You get three chances to ask for something, and then I won't listen anymore." This was very clever. She knew her son was going to whine, so she gave him permission to do it, but at the same time she set limits. Sometimes children don't know how to communicate their wants except by whining, so we can teach them alternatives. For instance, to a child crying "Cookie, cookie," you might say "I can hear you better when you use your big-girl voice" or "Can you say 'Please, Mom, can I have a cookie?'"

"I hate it when my house is a battleground," admitted Georgia, the soft-spoken mother of a four-year-old girl. "And things usually go okay, until I start to enforce rules." She laughed. "That's when I get into trouble. But I'm trying. For instance, I made a rule that Betsy could have a snack, like a cookie and milk, after school, until three-thirty. After that, it was too close to dinnertime. So, the other day, she came in from playing at four-thirty, and she wanted a cookie, and I said no because the rule was no cookies after three-thirty.

"Betsy threw a tantrum. She fell down on the floor and yelled, 'I hate you! I won't eat dinner, and I don't love you anymore.'

"I reached down and tried to put my arms around her,

pulling her up, but she pushed me away and screamed, 'I'm going to throw you in the garbage!'

"I know she was angry at me for not giving her a cookie. But I was trying not to get into a fight about it. I said nothing. I kept my mouth closed and didn't start with that old routine. You know—the whole thing about the way she was behaving, and she'd be sent to her room if she didn't stop, and so on. I said, 'You really like cookies, don't you?' She said yes, still crying a little. I said, 'I can see why. Cookies are yummy.' By now she was not crying, but looking at me a little curiously. I went on. 'Cookies are a nice treat to have before three-thirty, but not so good right before dinner. Tomorrow, let's be sure you remember to ask for your cookie on time. Why don't I set the alarm to be sure we both remember?' She said okay, a little pouty, and I said, 'I hope you don't throw me in the garbage, because if you do, I won't be here to set the alarm for your cookie time tomorrow.' That made her laugh. Crisis averted. She said, 'Okay, I won't,' and went off to play.

"There was a time when I would have given her a swat on the behind and sent her to her room if she had behaved that way. But this approach works better. I'm not giving in to her, but I'm not being mean to her either. And the whole evening isn't ruined over nothing."

Effective Crisis Management

Jane, a woman in my workshop, told the group of an incident she felt very good about. She was sitting in the living room with a friend having coffee. Her son, Jim, was jumping around, and he knocked a cup over onto Jane's beautiful Persian carpet. Jane, about to yell, swallowed and said, "We better sponge this up right away." Although she was tempted to scream at Jim for his carelessness, she held herself back. The other people in the workshop were amazed by Jane's self-restraint. Later, Jim said to his mother, "Mommy, I feel bad I spilled coffee all over your rug. I'm really sorry."

Consider what might have happened if, when the coffee spilled, Jane had jumped up out of her chair and started yelling: "Look what you've done now. You've ruined my best carpet. Why can't you be more careful? We'll never get the spot out. How many times have I told you not to jump around in the living room? Go to your room."

What might Jim's reaction have been? He would have felt angry, resentful, and embarrassed in front of his mother's friend. He might have yelled back "You care more about your stupid carpet than you care about me!" And he would have believed it at that moment. Although the incident had been an accident, Jane's anger would have made it seem as though he was bad.

I applauded Jane's handling of the situation, and I reminded the group, "As hard as it is to do this with your own children—and I'm the first to plead guilty to losing my temper with mine—it helps to recall how we respond when an adult spills liquid on the rug. We say 'Don't worry—here, let me help you clean it up.' " But with our children, we behave very differently. And when we respond by yelling, the problem intensifies instead of being resolved.

As adults, we have the ability to inject a little sanity into a situation when things feel out of control. Yet, when we're with children, we sometimes find ourselves acting their age or younger. When they are being childish, it's hard for us to act adultish. But when we can muster the skill to neutralize the situation, we feel much better. One way we can do this is by using humor.

One mother told me of an original solution she had discovered to get her dawdling three-year-old, Lily, out the door in the morning. "Lily loves fantasy and playacting, so I've been able to get her cooperation by personalizing her dolls, toys, clothes, and even parts of her body. Then I talk to her in 'that' voice—the voice of these objects. For example, one day we were running around, trying to get out of the house in time for nursery school, and Lily's party shoes were in the middle of the kitchen. I used to yell at her to put her shoes away, and she would say no or ignore me, and I would get mad. But that morning, I said in my most dramatic tone of voice, 'Lily, I hear the shoes saying something. Oh! It's 'We want to go back home and be with our friends in the closet. We're all alone here.' And in my 'shoe voice' I continued, 'Oh, yes, please can we go to the closet?' Now, when Lily doesn't want to put on her shoes, my shoe voice says, 'Please, please. We love your little feet. We wish we could be on your little feet.' And usually these games end up with Lily giggling and doing what I've asked instead of us both yelling and not getting anything done. It doesn't take any more time to play this game than it does to go through a series of noes. Lily will put on her shoes and say 'Shoes, do you like it now with my feet in your tummy?' And my shoe voice will answer, 'Oh, yes, thank you.' It's amazing what Lily will do for her clothes, toys, and teeth that she won't do for me."

This mother used her creativity to turn daily occasions for yelling into playacting. Another woman, Phyllis, talked about her efforts to keep her temper in check when her seven-year-old daughter dragged her feet in the morning and didn't want to get ready for school. Phyllis spoke of how hard she tried to be in what she called her "good mother mode" and have patience, because mornings were always very stressful in her house. When she heard Lily's mother's story, she shook her head enviously. "I would like to be that way with Sandy," she said. "But the truth is, even if we had four hours in the morning, she still wouldn't be ready." Phyllis kept trying, though, and one day she came to class with this incident, which had occurred the previous week. "I decided to use a little creativity and humor," she said and laughed. "But it didn't turn out as smoothly as I had hoped. I could tell that Sandy was going to give me a hard time about getting dressed, so I arranged all her clothes on the bed in the shape of a little girl. I took the pants, the turtleneck, the socks, the purse. I even put a balloon there for the head. Then I called Sandy into her room. Here's what happened."

PHYLLIS: Sandy, come and look at what I've got for you.

SANDY (coming into the room and seeing the girl shape on her bed): I don't like those pants. They're not the soft ones.

PHYLLIS (feeling a little deflated, but determined to be cheerful): Your sweats are in the wash. You can wear them tomorrow.

SANDY: I don't want them tomorrow. I want them today!

PHYLLIS: Come on, honey, let's go. We have to get ready.

SANDY: I don't want to go to school. I can't stand you.

PHYLLIS (still trying to be cheerful): You can't stand me!

SANDY: Yes, because you make me put on my clothes.

"At that point," Phyllis related, "all my good intentions flew right out the window, and I started my usual tirade about how it didn't matter what she wanted to do, she had to put on her clothes, and she'd better do it right away. The fun game I had planned fizzled, and it ended with Sandy messing up the girl shape on the bed and crying." Phyllis looked dejected. "I guess I'm a failure at being creative."

Not every technique works every time. Sometimes when

we bend over backward and make an extraordinary effort, as Phyllis did, and it fizzles, either we get madder or we feel like failures. There are no guarantees that our special efforts will work. And what works today may not work tomorrow. Face it—some days nothing works. Probably the best thing for Phyllis to have done would have been to say nothing and just leave the room for a few minutes, until she calmed down. If Sandy hadn't started getting dressed when Phyllis returned, she might have offered her daughter this choice: "Sandy, are you going to get dressed by yourself, or do you want Mommy to help you? We're leaving the house in twenty minutes." In other words, give Sandy a choice instead of giving her an order.

Children don't like to be ordered around, and how can we blame them? We don't order other adults around. I wouldn't say to another adult "Why did you put that wet glass on my coffee table? Were you brought up in a barn?" I would say "Here's a coaster." But we order our children around all the time. My son once said, "Whenever you tell me what to do, I want to do just the opposite." And he did, too! Then, of course, I would become angry. It's far more effective to state our requests in as neutral a tone as possible, instead of giving our children the impression that we have a personal vendetta against them. Rather than saying "Your clothes are always strewn on the floor! How many times have I told you to put them in the hamper? How can you be such a slob?" you could say "Dirty clothes belong in the hamper" or "Clothes that are not put in the hamper won't get washed." These responses are apt to elicit a more positive response from our children.

"My youngest daughter, Sue, who is eight, constantly finds a way to unnerve me in the morning," wrote Jill, a mother of three. "She refuses to get up without being yelled at, dawdles in the bathroom, can't decide what to wear, picks at her breakfast, and forgets where her backpack is. By the time we leave the house in the morning, I've usually screamed at least once, imposed a punishment that is so unrealistic that it usually is not carried out, and am suffering from a full-blown headache. Sue is hostile and surly or in tears. Here's an example of a typical morning."

MOM: Sue, it's time to get up.
SUE (pulling the covers over her head): Not yet.
MOM: Sue, get up now or you'll get a smack. [There's no sound from beneath the covers.] I mean now! I hate when you do this. You never get up when I call you. You always make me late.
SUE: I'm tired.
MOM: Well, then, you will go to bed at six-thirty tonight, and then we'll see if you're tired in the morning.

Jill went on to relate an escalating scene of Sue's not getting dressed, not brushing her teeth, and refusing to eat breakfast—ending with her and her daughter shrieking at each other.

"It is very hard for me to admit that for years this child has had a nagging, screeching shrew for a mother. I think I would move out if I were her."

Jill joined my class, and over time she began to institute some specific changes. One of these was an alarm clock set five minutes earlier than Sue needed to get up, so her daughter could have the experience of lounging in bed. "It hasn't always worked," said Jill, "but it has improved wake-up time drastically. The other morning, it was actually enlightening to wake Sue up." She recalled this scene.

MOM: The five extra minutes are up now. It's time to get out of bed.

SUE (from under the covers): I have a magic spell on me. To break the magic spell, you have to lie down next to me for two minutes.

MOM: Okay. [I lie down next to her and wait the two minutes.] Now the magic spell is broken. Arise, my lovely princess. You are free from the wicked witch's spell.

SUE (laughing as she bounds out of bed): Oh, Mommy, you are so silly.

Agnes, one of my students, learned to keep her sense of humor and get her preadolescent son, Craig, to deal with the messes he left throughout the house. She brought to class two dialogues she had written. One represented the way she handled the situation before taking the workshop, and the other represented a new technique she tried that worked more effectively.

Precourse dialogue:

AGNES: What kind of a slob are you? I work hard all day and come home to this? I'm not your maid. Clean up right now. Start in one room, and go through every room where you made a mess in this house.

CRAIG: Oh, shit, Ma! Look at your room. Look at your dresser, you call that neat? Ha! Why are you always criticizing me when you can't keep things straight yourself?

AGNES: You've got a lot of nerve to speak to me that way! Now you're dirty *and* rude. Clean up now, or you'll be sorry.

Postcourse letter to Craig:

> Dear Craig,
> The maids in this establishment are on strike. Consequently,
> we need your help. The vacuum is plugged in and all ready
> for you. We know you'll do a fine job. When you finish vac-
> uuming your room, please wash your breakfast dishes. Then
> you need to pick up your wet towels from the bathroom floor
> and hang up the clothes in your bedroom. The management
> certainly appreciates this help.
>
> Love,
Mom and Dad

"He didn't do everything on the list, but he did most of
it, and he laughed about it. Now, sometimes when his room
is a mess, he will say 'I guess the management would like
me to clean up.' "

Another parent related an occasion where she was able
to achieve a breakthrough in the nightly battle waged with
her seven-year-old, Stephanie, over bedtime.

STEPHANIE: It's not fair that I have to go to bed at seven-
   thirty. All the kids in my class get to stay up later. I'm
   the only one who has to go to bed this early. They get
   to stay up until nine.
MOM: Their parents let them stay up that late? Well, I do
   what I think is best for my own children. [Then she
   deliberately changes the mood.] If you could stay up as
   late as you wanted, until what time would you stay up,
   and what would you do?
STEPHANIE: I'd stay up real late and watch TV all night,
   and read books and be real happy.

MOM: Okay, I'll tell you what. You pick a night when you can stay up real late, on a weekend, and we'll plan for that special night.

STEPHANIE: I want to stay up late on March nineteenth, on my birthday.

MOM (smiling, because the date was six months away): Okay, let's check and see if March nineteenth is on a weekend.

Marcy elicited Stephanie's cooperation by giving her some control over her life, and making her feel that her wants would not always be met with a series of noes.

Even as I suggest techniques to help alleviate the daily battles, I warn parents that these techniques do not work every time with every child. But knowing that there are potential solutions helps parents feel less helpless against the barrage of mundane issues—if one solution does not work, another can be tried. Sometimes just the realization that other parents share the same dilemmas goes a long way toward diminishing the anger and frustration people feel about their own struggles with parenting.

3

Who's the Boss?

Is this an examination? Can't you understand there are some parts of my life I want to keep for myself? Do you have to know everything? Next time I go to the bathroom, I'll write a report.   —an indignant teenager

"I'm the boss. Someday when you're grown up and have children of your own, you can be the boss. But for now, I'm in charge, and you'll do what I say." Joanne heard her own mother's often-repeated words ring in her ears as she sat gloomily in the kitchen and waited for her son, Steve, to arrive home. Some boss I am, she thought bitterly. Her ten-year-old constantly tested the limits she imposed, expressing open defiance of her wishes. Just that morning she had told him, in no uncertain terms, that he was to come directly home from school that day because she needed his help with some errands that had to be done before the family's vacation the following week.

"Ah, Mom," he had protested. "The guys are going to ride their bikes after school. Can't I go with them?"

"Steve, I need you home," she said firmly, and thought that was the end of it. But now it was nearly five, and Steve still had not arrived home. Once again, as had been happening so often lately, he had defied her. She felt hot with rage, planning how she would punish her son. But deep down, she knew that the punishment wouldn't solve anything. Her son had made it clear that no matter how often he was punished, he would do what he pleased.

"I don't want to be an ogre," Joanne said, when she later told me about the experience. "But I feel that Steve forces my hand. If I don't punish him, he'll think he can get away with murder. But the punishment never stops him from doing it again. I'm fit to be tied over this."

I asked her what happened when her son arrived home that day, and she sighed heavily. "He got home about a quarter after five, and walked in the door all innocent. As soon as he said 'Hi, Mom,' I erupted like Mount Saint Helens. 'Where have you been?' He looked at me like I was a maniac, and very casually said he was out riding bikes with his friends. I pounded my fist on the table and yelled, 'I told you to come right home after school today. I will not have you defy me this way.' He tried to tell me he'd forgotten, but that just made me more angry. I called him a liar, and I guess I used a few other choice epithets, too. When my husband walked in the door, I was still screaming."

"What was your husband's reaction?"

"Oh, Frank hates it when Steve and I have arguments, and he usually ends up blaming me, as though he thinks I should be able to handle things better. Maybe he's right, but I wish he would stick up for me more. That night he got disgusted and said, 'Are you two at it again?'—as though we were both his children. Later that night, when I was calmer, I tried to talk to Frank about how frustrating it was to have Steve challenge my authority. He thought I was making too much of it, and he said—this really hurt!— 'Something's wrong if you, an adult woman of thirty-two, can't even control a ten-year-old kid.' You can imagine who was the next target of my fury!"

Of course it's frustrating to have a child defy our authority; it can make us feel helpless. Joanne needs to find a quiet time when she is not feeling so angry to discuss with her husband how important it is for them to present a united front to their son. She also needs to realize that kids will test authority—there's no way to stop that. The idea that a parent is "boss" gets challenged in a thousand ways, and just knowing that it's natural can help dissipate some of the helplessness and anger we feel.

Joanne's sense of anger and helplessness often was reflected in the voices of parents who complained that they could not control their children. More than half of those who answered my survey wrote that these power struggles constituted their most frustrating and anger-producing moments:

I say one thing and my son totally tunes me out and does exactly what he pleases.

My children don't listen to me. They either ignore me or they're making so much noise, I have to scream to be heard.

It makes me furious when I have asked the children several times to stop fighting or do their chores, and I get no cooperation.

My teenage daughter states her opinions, which disagree with mine, and then proceeds to do what she wants. She'll say "It's my life" or "It's my body, not yours" or the most frightening of all, "You can't stop me."

I will explain carefully and logically what needs to be done in certain circumstances, but they won't take my advice. It bugs me that they don't give me any credit for knowing what I'm talking about.

My older son will *immediately* repeat the behavior I have *just* finished asking him to stop.

Wise-ass comments from my second child really bug me. I say no to some request, and he says, "Fine!" in a sarcastic tone of voice.

Our six-year-old has started calling my husband and me "fart face." He gets very angry when he doesn't get his way, and this is how he expresses his feelings.

The battle for control is an age-old issue between parents and their children. It's infuriating to lay down the law, only to have it broken again and again. Understandably, parents grow angry when they can't control their children. Perhaps viewed objectively, we can see why children have to assert themselves, just as parents have to make rules. But that doesn't make it any easier to know what to do in the heat of the moment when our child says "No!"

It offends our sensibilities as parents to be confronted with the fact that we are not the all-powerful bosses of our children. They tell us this themselves. "You are not the boss over me!" is the favorite parental button pusher of many children. What we want is for them to understand that our judgment is based on years of experience, that what we say is the rule, and that they should do as we tell them because we love them and have greater wisdom than they do. (We also want them to be grateful to us for all the efforts we make for them.) When they refuse to accept our restrictions, we become frustrated and enraged, and threaten, punish, hit, or—just as ineffective—back down or give in.

Rebecca was worried about how defiant her son, Ron, was becoming. "When Ron was little, we never hit him or disciplined him very firmly. He was such a delightful kid, and when he'd act up, we'd handle it somehow. But my mother always used to say 'When he gets older, he's going to shit on you.' And now he's seven and he's getting very rambunctious. Whenever he's really fresh, those words of hers come back to haunt me—'he's shitting on you.' Then I think ahead to when he'll be eleven or thirteen or fifteen, and I wonder how I'm going to manage him. I start feeling guilty that we haven't disciplined him more firmly, and that we didn't spank him when he was younger. It's such a disappointment, because until a few months ago, he was easy as pie. Carl and I felt we were doing everything right. Now Mom's warning seems to be coming true."

It's pretty common for parents to let their imagination run away with them, as Rebecca's did. You think "My God, if he's this way now, what's he going to be like in five years?" But what Rebecca described is fairly typical behavior for a seven-year-old, who is busy testing his wings. It doesn't mean that Rebecca should ignore his behavior, but neither should she let her mother's comment poison her view of what's really going on with Ron.

In the workshop, we talked more about Rebecca's own childhood, and she told me her mother was a very strict disciplinarian. "We kids would never even think about talking back to her. We were always afraid of how she might react, and she spanked us a lot. I wanted things to be different for Ron. I thought if he had more freedom to express himself, he wouldn't be so defiant. Now I'm afraid I was wrong."

Many of today's parents, who have rejected the punitive environments of their own upbringings are, like Rebecca, confused and disappointed when their children still express

anger and defiance. They had hoped that their more benevolent approach to parenting would do away with these
inevitable power struggles.

Other parents simply cannot bear to listen to words of
anger coming from their children's mouths. It makes them
feel that they have lost all authority. How dare a child
speak to them that way! If they had ever spoken to *their*
parents like that, they would have been severely punished.

But it is normal for children to test our limits—both in
words and actions. Establishing independence from adult
authority is a healthy way for children to find their own
styles. The question is how can parents walk the tricky line
between allowing their children to express their feelings
while still asserting their authority as parents, and setting
necessary limits. Some of the central dilemmas include the
following:

How to set appropriate limits—when to insist on nonnegotiable rules and when to be flexible and negotiate
compromises. How to involve children in an agreement
over important things, and how to negotiate the flexible
areas.

How to react when children get angry and say things
like "I hate you," "You're not my friend," or (as one
parent reported) "I'd like to throw you in the garbage."

How to respond when children verbally defy authority,
saying "No, I won't" or "You can't make me."

What consequences to impose when children disobey
and go ahead with a forbidden action.

These are issues of authority that virtually every parent
grapples with. Those who believe they have "earned" their

children's obedience, by virtue of their having achieved parenthood status, are constantly confronted by the hard truth that children will challenge their authority every step of the way.

Who's in Charge?

Control first becomes an issue when our children are still toddlers, at the point when they get past the innocence of infancy. The first year they are helpless and totally dependent upon on us, and the next they've learned how to say "No!"—which signals their initial declaration of independence. They love that word because it expresses all their sense of emerging identity and separateness. At this stage, power struggles occur constantly, over everything from spitting out food to toileting to refusing to hold our hand when crossing the street.

During the years when a child is first pulling away, it is very hard for parents to deal with the constant barrage of noes and the refusal to go along with our plans. One mother told me in despair, "Jack will never be toilet trained! He'll be wearing diapers to college!" I laughed, because I think all of us who have had children felt the same way when faced with their newfound defiance. Over the years, thousands of parents have complained to me about their toddlers' and preschoolers' stubbornness and willfulness.

"It's frustrating," Jack's mother said. "Every night before bed, it's the same thing. I tell him he has to stay in the bathroom until he goes, and he stays in there for what seems like hours, repeating 'No go, no go' and not producing even a trickle. Finally, I'm worn out and I send him to bed. An hour later, he's crying because he's soaking wet."

I suggested to this mother that she might have more success if she stopped making going to the toilet a power struggle. Once you say "You're going to sit there until you go," you've lost the battle. Because I suspect Jack is 90 percent toilet trained, and now he's using it as a weapon to gain control.

You need to be worried about the toddler who is *not* curious, messy, touching everything. But it's exhausting to be constantly saying "No!" and hearing it said back to you. Find out what happens when you try to use yes first—for example:

"I want candy!"
"Yes, you can have candy as soon as lunch is over."

"Can I play with my bubbles?"
"Yes, when we go into the yard."

"Me wanna go out now."
"Yes, we're going after you put on your socks and shoes."

You might find that your child, who is already geared up to fight your no, will respond more cooperatively when he or she hears yes, even if the underlying refusal is still there.

Toddlers and preschoolers may throw frequent tantrums, but they need to know that, if they lose control, someone will be there to steady them and to help them set boundaries. In spite of their bottomless reserves of contradictory behavior, children generally feel most secure when they know there is someone who will establish the limits that they are incapable of setting for themselves. (That is why my first response to parents is only half-facetious when they ask what to do when a child has a tantrum: "First, try not to have a tantrum too!")

Humor is a powerful way of defusing power struggles, distracting a child, and "joining" rather than offering head-on opposition. One of my students demonstrated this with a story. Dad was washing his four-year-old daughter's hair, amid loud protests. He managed to finish, in spite of the complaints and tears. She was furious! Touching her shiny hair, she said vehemently, "Now I'm going to get mud and pour it all over my head!" Instead of responding "If you do, we'll have to wash it again," Dad said, "Oh no! Let's get elephant pee-pee and pour it all over your head!" She laughed uproariously and climbed out of the tub.

Forcing Submission

"How many of you remember physical punishment being used as a means of control when you were kids?" I asked my class one day. Most of the parents raised their hands.

Tom, a young father of two preschoolers, was clearly reliving his fury as he recalled the night when he was sixteen and his father slapped him across the face. "I felt so violated—so *hurt*—that for the first time in my life, I hit him back. The incident changed our relationship. For years, I had suppressed my rage. And for sixteen years, he had spanked and slapped me regularly. It was the first time I said 'Hey, you don't have a right to do that.'"

Sometimes, when all other attempts to assert authority fail, parents feel pushed to the point where they see no other choice but to use physical force. The subject of hitting and spanking is an ongoing topic in my parent groups. Many parents are reluctant to hit their kids, but they often wonder whether there are times when it's the only thing left that works.

"My parents spanked me," said Irene, the mother of a four-year-old girl and an infant boy. "Now that I think about it, the only way my parents knew how to deal with me when I wasn't being good was to yell and hit. I'm horrified when I hear myself screaming and realize I sound just like my mother. But at least I don't hit."

"So what *is* a good punishment for a child who refuses to obey?" asked Tom.

I laughed. I get this question all the time, and I usually take the fifth. There's no simple answer. Some children are devastated by our merely telling them we're angry or disappointed; others can be spanked over and over again without it making any difference in their behavior. I remember one woman telling me "My mother could discipline me with her right eyebrow." But one question you might ask yourselves is "Would I punish the same way if I were calm?" The best time to punish is not when we're at our maddest, but that's usually when we do it.

Chris, who had regaled the class with many stories of her "little monster," Bart, who was four, shrugged helplessly. "Some behavior is simply unacceptable, like Bart's habit of using vulgar words, and I feel I have no choice but to punish him harshly so he knows he can't do it. I don't like to spank, but I use other methods, such as washing his mouth out with soap when he uses dirty words." Chris related the following incident:

CHRIS: Bart, if you say one more dirty word, I'm going to wash your mouth out with soap.

BART: Fucking asshole!

CHRIS (with raised voice): Bart, I mean it! Stop saying those disgusting words.

BART: Fucking asshole! Fucking asshole!

CHRIS: Okay, you asked for it. (Gets a bar of Ivory soap, puts the soapy water in her hand, and pushes it into his mouth.)

"How many times have you washed Bart's mouth out with soap?" I asked.

"I've had to do it several times, and I'm determined to keep doing it until he gets the message," she replied firmly.

"What if he never gets the message? What if he learns to love the taste of soap?" I asked, half-teasing. Many parents believe that punishing, if you do it enough, will eventually encourage a child to change or to cooperate. But Chris washes Bart's mouth out with soap, and he continues to use vulgar words. And Tom remembers how his father's spankings only made him bitter and generated thoughts of revenge. The problem with physical punishment is not just that the punishment might not work—it might even backfire. It's also that when your children defy you and you get really mad at them, you may, at that moment, *want* to inflict a little pain and make them feel bad. You want to hurt them. Maybe not throw them out the window but, as the phrase goes, *teach them a lesson.* Chris thinks that soap in the mouth is a pretty awful experience. She might say "This will teach you." But what is she actually teaching him? Do you hear a kind of revenge implicit in her statement? When we really get mad, many of us have a powerful urge to get even. We want to twist the knife or let our kids feel the same pain they're making us feel. I believe it would be more effective to say very firmly "No swearing in this house." Or "Those words are totally unacceptable." Then he might go out in the yard and call you names under his breath, but that's okay. It also helps to realize that preschoolers like to use bathroom language for shock value— and it works because we are shocked.

When their authority is challenged, even in small ways, some parents feel pushed up against a wall. They might start out by calmly making a very simple request, but when results don't follow, the tendency is to up the ante or use more force. The mother of a six-year-old related this story.

CELESTE: Avery, your teeth need brushing.
AVERY: I won't brush my teeth.

"He takes his toothbrush and throws it into the bathtub. I'm getting furious, because this is a regular scene. I'm trying to suppress the anger which is building up. I retrieve the toothbrush and hand it to him."

CELESTE: You don't like brushing your teeth, but they need to be brushed. Now do it.

"He throws the toothbrush on the floor and says 'No!' I grit my teeth and feel I have to see this problem through. Avery has been to the dentist, and he has cavities."

CELESTE: I'm really, really angry. This has to be done, and if you won't cooperate, I'll spank you.
AVERY: No, I won't.

"So I spank him once hard, and he cries hysterically. Then he says, 'I'm running away. I hate hate hate you!' Then he runs out the door. I realized my spanking was a knee-jerk reaction to feeling helpless. But I just didn't know what else to do."

Celeste's good intentions, as well as her vision of herself as a "reasonable mother," flew out the window when Avery stubbornly refused to brush his teeth. All parents harbor a hope that, once their children understand the reasons behind the rules, they will become cooperative. But people—and that includes children—don't always do what they know is best for them. In the following dialogue, supplied by a mother in my class, Tristan knew full well why he had to wear his retainer. But his knowing it, and even his agreement that he didn't want crooked teeth, didn't bring him any closer to doing it.

FRAN: Tristan, you didn't put your retainer back in your mouth after dinner. That's the twentieth time this week!

TRISTAN: I hate this retainer!

FRAN (getting so angry that she throws the retainer across the room): Now, look what you made me do!

TRISTAN (crying): You broke it!

FRAN: I didn't mean to break it, but it makes me so mad when you refuse to put it back in your mouth. Dammit, you know you have to wear it.

Fran was embarrassed as she related this incident to the group. It's easy to see that nothing was accomplished in this scenario. It's true that sometimes our kids can reduce us to their level or below. In her anger, Fran blamed Tristan for her own action, and probably scared him a little, too, when he saw he had the power to drive his mother into such a frenzy. I discussed with Fran how she might handle this problem differently, since it was unresolved and bound to recur. The next week, she related to the class the following dialogue.

FRAN: Tristan, your retainer is still on the table. It belongs in your mouth after dinner. [Stated as a fact, not an accusation.]

TRISTAN: I hate that retainer!

FRAN: I know. It's not fun to have a retainer in your mouth. [Acknowledges the legitimacy of his feelings.] Why do you think you have to wear it?

TRISTAN: So my teeth won't be crooked. But I still don't like it.

FRAN: Yes, it's hard to do some things even when they're supposed to be good for us.

"I also called the orthodontist and asked him to talk to Tristan about the importance of wearing the retainer, the next time he came for a checkup," Fran said.

Fran tried to act as Tristan's ally in this situation, while at the same time making it clear that he was expected to wear the retainer. It was a revelation for her to discover that it was possible to assert authority without relying on threats or punishment. And Tristan's reaction was more cooperative as a result.

When our children defy us or behave unacceptably, often our least loving behavior comes through. I think all of us have two sides. We have a loving side and a vengeful, not-so-loving side. If a stranger cuts in front of us on the highway and we almost have an accident, we feel great if we can tell that person off, using our choicest vulgar epithets. But when we tell off our children, the words usually end up being hurtful—and we don't feel relieved. We feel out of control and guilty. It's not the same as the stranger on the highway.

Parents always ask me what I think about spanking, and I tell them that if spanking worked, we'd only have to do it once. Basically, spanking is nothing more than a big person using force against a smaller person. It can do damage to your child, and in the long run it doesn't work. You may be lucky and succeed in getting your child to obey you or stop whining or do what you want him to for a moment. But you've created hard feelings in the process, and you haven't set an example that you want your child to follow in the future.

A Matter of Trust

Power struggles occur at every stage of development, but we may be most aware of them at the toddler and adolescent stages. These are two transitional periods when achieving a separate identity is a priority for our children.

Parents of teenagers have a particular challenge on their hands, because testing parental authority is practically a full-time job for teens. I remember how scary it was for me as my two sons reached their teen years and began severely testing the limits their father and I imposed. On the one hand, I realized that this was healthy. We refer to teenagers as "young adults," and we expect them to start thinking and acting independently, as part of the process of separation. On the other hand, I still viewed my sons as terribly vulnerable—especially so, since I was aware of the increasing influence of racing hormones and peer pressure. I was fearful that they would make mistakes that would have terrible consequences.

Trust is a big issue between teenagers and their parents. While our children are demanding more freedom, at the same time they are asking us to trust them. We are torn between assuring them that we trust them and recognizing that trust cannot mean giving away our right to impose the limits they need. Sometimes they try to get around our authority by lying, and when we catch our children lying, we immediately want to say "Aha! Now you know why I can't trust you." Instead of hurling accusations, sometimes we have to listen to what they are telling us when they are dishonest.

In *Why Kids Lie*, author Paul Ekman turned over a chapter to his son, Tom, who wrote "A Teenager's Views on Lying"—providing a rare view inside the mind of a teenager.

The young Ekman acknowledged that kids most often lie to their parents to avoid punishment or a lecture. But he also pointed out additional reasons. "I think kids lie about other things for which they would not get punished because they want to keep a little bit of privacy," he wrote. "There are things that kids want to keep to themselves, such as things they are embarrassed about, things that they are ashamed of, and things that they simply do not want their parents to know about."

Parents find themselves engaged in the delicate balance between respecting this legitimate need for privacy and at the same time being effective guardians. For Tom Ekman also admits, "Just about everyone I know has lied about homework many times . . . and just about everyone I know has lied about cheating and work done in school."

Karen's fourteen-year-old son, Billy, had been lying to her lately about small things: "I called you at the office to tell you I'd be home late, but you weren't there" or "I'm too sick to go to school." Karen was concerned, not because the lies were so severe but because she felt they were creating a breakdown in their trust. She thought carefully about how to approach Billy without putting him on the defensive, while still emphasizing the values of mutual trust in their relationship.

KAREN: I have something very serious to talk to you about.
BILLY: What?
KAREN: I'm feeling really insecure about whether you're telling me the truth lately, and I'm feeling that my trust in you is slipping away.
BILLY (immediately defensive): When did I lie? When did I lie?

KAREN: The details are not important right now. What's important is that I feel I can't trust what you say to me, and I need that to change.

BILLY: Just tell me one time.

KAREN: I'm willing to accept some of the responsibility for what's going on, because I think one reason you don't tell the truth is because of the way I react. Maybe you're scared to tell me the truth.

BILLY: Yeah, you do yell a lot when I tell you things.

KAREN: I intend to stop that.

BILLY (surprised): Why?

KAREN: Because I need you to tell me the truth so badly that I'm willing to change my reaction and give up the relief I feel when I yell.

BILLY: I can tell you the truth about some things, but other things are too private.

KAREN: I understand. But instead of lying, just tell me you don't feel comfortable answering the question, and I'll try to respect that.

BILLY: Sometimes I do worry about telling you the truth, because I'm afraid you'll crack down and put more limits on my life.

KAREN: I can see why that would make it tempting to lie. But since our relationship is based on trust, all I can tell you is that I will try not to use that information against you.

BILLY: In that case, I need to tell you something. Remember when I went to bed early last Saturday night, telling you I had a stomachache? Well, what really happened was I went to the mall. I know I'm not supposed to go there alone, and that's why I didn't tell you. This gang of kids with knives started hassling me because they thought I was this kid from another school. They pushed me around. Finally, I showed them my ID to prove to them I wasn't the kid they were looking for. But I was too scared to tell you before.

This conversation was very revealing. Karen discovered that, contrary to what she had thought, Billy wasn't lying in order to "get away with murder," but because he was afraid she would interfere in situations he wanted to handle himself or that she would put limits on his life—a common reason why kids lie to their parents. Although he had been terrified at the incident, he was afraid to tell his mother for fear she would restrict his freedom.

Karen was skillful in the way she handled this situation. She gave Billy the opportunity to be more open, without fear of repercussions, and I admired the enormous self-control she exhibited in maintaining her calm, especially after her son told her of his frightening encounter at the mall. It's a delicate balance parents must negotiate between letting go and maintaining control. As our children get older, we know that once they walk out the door, we don't have a lot of power. And we're all too aware that there can be terrible consequences to the actions of teenagers. But much as we'd like to, we cannot always be there to protect our children from the outside world.

One common refrain of teenagers is to say "I didn't ask you because I knew you wouldn't let me." This infuriates parents, who, logically, consider this to be a direct act of defiance. Lisa related in my workshop the story of what happened when her fourteen-year-old daughter, Carla, came home from school one day with a second hole pierced in her ear.

LISA: I can't believe you had your ear pierced with a second hole! You never asked me if it was okay.

CARLA: I always wanted two holes, so I finally did it. I knew if I asked you, you'd say no, so I didn't ask.

LISA: Not asking me because you knew what my response would be is the same thing as defying me. It's the same as lying. Now I feel as though I can't trust you alone in the mall, so I will not permit you to go there for the next month.

CARLA: I figured you would punish me, but I thought about it and decided I wanted to do it, even though I knew you'd be mad. Anyway, I don't see what's so bad about getting a second hole in my ear. Everyone else has one.

LISA: That's not the point. The point is that you deliberately sidestepped my authority. You will have to show me that I can trust you again by behaving responsibly before you will be permitted to go back to the mall with your friends.

When Lisa related this incident to my workshop group, she was feeling very frustrated. "I realized that I have very little control over Carla's actions," she said. "She knew she'd get in trouble, but she did it anyway. I feel completely helpless."

We all sympathize with Lisa's frustration. Carla is at an age where it's important to establish a unique physical style—and usually that style is one that parents find most distasteful. Allowing her to have a second hole pierced in her ear or wear ragged jeans or put on garish purple eyeshadow is relatively harmless, and enables a teenager to have some control. I think we need to make a distinction here. There's a difference between setting limits in areas involving safety, destructive or self-destructive behavior, and values, and setting limits on choices in dress and appearance.

But Lisa still was troubled. "Carla is a pretty good kid," she said, "but I don't want to be a wimp. If I let her think she can walk all over me, I'm afraid one thing will lead to another, and more serious problems will take place. Right now, my daughter is going through a stage when she doesn't want to let me know anything at all. So how can I know when a more important issue arises? I'm afraid to trust her too much."

Lisa is right. This is tricky business. As a parent, you have a responsibility for your child's security—and you need to insist on certain rules of safety, such as always having the phone number where she is or insisting that she be home by a certain hour. And this has less to do with trust than an awareness of what can happen out in the world. As one mother told her teenage son, "*You* I trust—it's the crazies out there I'm worried about." It is best to look at each situation and decide when it's important for you to intercede. It has been my experience that when parents of teenagers really want to influence them in issues related to sexuality, drinking, drugs, and other major issues, we can do so more effectively if we let up somewhat on the minor issues, such as keeping a clean room, dressing a certain way, or using swear words.

Letting Go

Battles over control are really the outgrowth of the struggle between our desire to hold on to our children for as long as possible and the necessity, finally, of letting go. Parents often express their ambivalence about this—saying, for example, "I try to foster their independence, yet I get really angry when they stand up to me" or "I want my daughter to make her own decisions, but I wish she would listen to and respect my suggestions."

Sandra, who had been in my workshop for several years, spoke of the pain she felt as she watched her sixteen-year-

old daughter growing away from her. The process of separation led to many battles. One day in the workshop,
Sandra was feeling particularly miserable. "We had a big
blow-up this morning," she said. "I did pretty well. For a
change, I didn't raise my voice. But I felt very hurt." I
asked Sandra to tell the class what had happened.

"I had asked Kim to come home right after school to
baby-sit for her younger brother, and she grew furious," said
Sandra. "When I insisted, she threatened to slap my face
and used the f-word. I just said, 'Your talking like that will
get you nowhere. I don't like the language you're using.'
But I stayed calm, and she left for school in a huff, slamming
the door behind her. Even though I feel kind of bad about
what happened, I know I handled my anger pretty well. A
year ago, I would have been completely destroyed over what
happened this morning. Now, I pick up the pieces and keep
going, thinking tomorrow is another day."

"So, you don't need Kim to like you anymore," I noted.

Sandra grew thoughtful. "I guess you're right. I don't
need that anymore."

"And you don't need to like her behavior," I added. "It
sounds like your daughter isn't very likable right now, and
you're working on not letting her provoke you in areas you
can't change."

"I admit that I'm bitterly disappointed in her right now,
for several reasons," Sandra said. "For one thing, she's
madly in love with a boy who is the last person on earth
any parent would pick for their daughter. The very last!
And a year ago, I would have said 'My God, what are we
going to do?' This year, I'm able to think maybe the experience will be good for her. Maybe she'll learn something
from it."

It isn't easy to see the formerly loving child who once
curled up in our laps turn into a surly stranger who cannot

spare us a kind word. One mother, managing to laugh through her hurt, observed wryly, "When my son walks in the house, I say 'How was your day?' and he responds, 'Get off my back!' " Another mother was equally taken aback when she called, as her daughter was going out the door, "Have a good time," and her daughter angrily replied, "Stop telling me what to do!"

A parent in one of my groups voiced a common sentiment when she admitted, "I was so thrilled when my daughter was born. For years, I've looked forward to the time when she would be old enough so that we could really share intimacies. I imagined myself telling her stories from my youth, and giving her advice about clothes and boys. But she barely speaks to me, and the last thing in the world she seems to want is my advice."

Like Sandra, this mother was pained by the recognition that her daughter didn't think of her as a friend. Her frustration with her daughter's reluctance to confide in her only made the mother question her more at every opportunity. She constantly tried to find ways to break through her daughter's obstinate silence.

"The other day we were sitting in the kitchen, one of the rare times recently when we were together. She had recently started going out with her first boyfriend, and I casually asked her how things were going with Sean. She gave me a very annoyed look, said 'Fine' in an abrupt voice, and then left the room. I followed her and started yelling about how I was sick of being treated like dirt, and I didn't deserve it. I was so hurt and furious, but my yelling only made her disgusted. She went into her room and slammed the door."

"How did you feel?" I asked.

"Close to tears," she admitted. "Shut out. Abandoned." She shook her head. "Nothing seems to work."

"Do you remember how you used to feel about your mother when you were a teenager?" I asked.

She thought for a moment, and a slow look of recognition spread across her face. "I did everything I could to make my mother mad. She wanted desperately to know everything, and I wouldn't tell her. If she'd try to give me advice or criticize me, I'd use my most sarcastic tone and say 'Thank you *so* much for sharing that with me.' I guess it's natural, but it hurts when you're the one on the other end."

It is easy to sympathize with this mother's feelings. She offered friendship and a listening ear only to be rejected by her daughter. She was like the father who described his thirteen-year-old daughter who "went to bed as Cinderella and woke up as Godzilla." This father wailed, "I want to quit being a parent!" Parents who long to be their teenagers' friends and confidants must remember that friendship implies a certain amount of equality, which simply does not exist between parent and child. Our children rightly experience us as the rule makers and limit setters in their lives—roles that are not always consistent with friendship. Sometimes we have to accept that loving our children means taking a backseat to the main drama of their lives. Clinical psychologist Jonathan Bloom-Feshbach notes in his paper *Growing Pains,* published by the Institute for Mental Health Initiatives,

There is necessary tension and struggle in the natural process of separation and individuation. On one hand, children seek a separate, self-directed identity. They want to make their own decisions and do things by themselves. On the other hand, this freedom and responsibility exacts a toll. Relinquishing some degree of emotional attachment and parental reliance is painful. Children present their parents with mixed messages: wanting help yet refusing assistance, desiring closeness yet seeking distance, expressing love and affection yet in the next breath professing anger or even hatred.

As Haim Ginott has observed in *Between Parent and Teenager*, "As parents, our need is to be needed. As children, their need is not to need us. To let go when we want to hold on requires utmost generosity and love."

4

Kids Versus Kids

Why don't we put her in the oven and pretend she's a snack?
—three-year-old, about the new baby

"My kids hate each other," said Maureen miserably. "No matter what I do, they're at each other's throats from the time they wake up in the morning until the time they go to sleep at night."

Maureen, the mother of two boys, seven and four, and a girl, ten, has been taking my workshop for three years. "I feel that I've come so far in the way I relate to my children," she said. "But this is the one area where I can't seem to make any headway. Not only do my seven-year-old and ten-year-old have a bad habit of fighting with each other, but they also gang up on the youngest, and then it's really awful."

I asked Maureen to describe a typical scene. "What bothers me the most is when their behavior seems to be just plain mean," she said. "For instance, I'll hear the two older children teasing their little brother to tears, saying things like 'Tommy is a turkey, Tommy is a turkey,' until Tommy starts crying. Then they'll go, 'Baby, baby, crybaby.' If I intervene, it gets worse for Tommy. But I can't stand not

71

to intervene because it makes me feel bad to see this little child so miserable. It's wrong for my children to be deliberately cruel. This is not what I expected when I decided to have three children. I wanted them to love each other, and I don't know why they don't."

Maureen feels guilty and helpless, and she resents her children for acting mean to each other. I tell her that she's right to want to discourage cruelty. But at the same time, she needs to accept the fact that she won't always be able to make her children kind to one another. Sibling rivalry drives parents crazy, but it is a natural state of affairs. "The home is the setting in which both the most ardent ties of love are formed and the deepest hatreds simmer," write Herbert S. Strean and Lucy Freeman in their book *Raising Cain.* "There is probably no more intense relationship than the sibling bond, except the bond between child and parent."

Their point is a good one, because families are made up of our most intimate relationships, and part of being intimate is to argue sometimes, become irritated, disagree, and get angry. But at the same time, many parents, like Maureen, fear that if they accept the anger and the fights that occur among their children, and don't try to intercede, they can forget about having a loving home. They find it hard to accept the inevitable—that children will argue, accuse, tease, and fight in a never-ending cycle. Any transgression (or imaginary transgression) can set them off: "You breathed on me!" "Mommy, Harold is looking at me." "She messed up my models." "Your foot is in my space." And the age-old refrain of all siblings, "It's not fair!"

"I know my children love each other, deep down," one mother, Jan, told me. Then she laughed. "*Very* deep down. The problem is that none of this love ever seems to rise to the surface. Why do they resent each other so much? Why are they always so mad at each other?" Most parents don't feel that it helps much to be told that sibling rivalry is a normal part of family life. "As their mother, it is my responsibility to guide them, to teach them kindness to others," said one mother. "When I see them being unkind to one another, I feel that I have to step in. Unfortunately, my intervention and my preaching seem to fall on deaf ears."

If you have more than one child, you can probably identify with Jan's dilemma. You're sick and tired of your children always fighting and arguing. It's so delightful to see siblings playing nicely together, sticking up for one another, and being loving and caring. But more often, it seems that they are at war.

Many of the parents in my survey described deep frustration and anger when they considered the hurtful feelings and actions their children expressed toward one another.

They interrupt my peace. When I want to sit down and relax for a few minutes, their fighting makes relaxation impossible.

Sometimes they physically hurt each other and appear to be out of control. I often feel that my younger one needs my protection, but when I say anything, the older one accuses me of favoritism. It shouldn't be this way in my home.

My older daughter will say to her sister, when the younger one has just received a compliment, "What's so great about that? I can do . . ." and then go on to brag about one of her accomplishments. It hurts me to see how defeated my younger child becomes when she is criticized by her older sister.

My children are always at each other's throats. They can be so mean! I almost don't recognize them during those moments. And all three of them want to have the last word. Their arguments can go on for hours, and the worst thing is when they call on me for help against one another.

We'll set aside special family time to be together, then they'll spend all of it bickering and teasing one another.

There have been times when my daughter pushed her younger brother so hard that he has fallen and hurt his head. I'm afraid she may seriously harm him.

I am always playing the role of the policeman, trying to break up fights. I'm so tired of the constant conflicts.

It makes me angry when my eldest is mean to his younger brother. He's always putting him down, and then the younger one gets even by messing up his brother's favorite models and baseball cards.

The most common statement parents make about their children's battles is "It shouldn't be this way." They long for a cure to the endless squabbling, and they become angry when nothing they try seems to work.

Why Siblings Fight

Parents driven to their wits' end over constant squabbling often find themselves shouting futile orders that fall on determinedly deaf ears:

Play nicely.
Knock it off.
Cool it.

You two behave.
Be good.
Get along.
Stop that fighting.
Be nice.
Act your age.

These admonitions are far too vague to be useful. And they place parents in the position of joining the fray rather than dissipating the anger.

It helps to take a step back and evaluate what is happening when children fight. It is a hard subject to be objective about, since most parents long desperately for their children to be friends and for their families to behave like loving units. They are fearful that there are dark forces at work. "It depresses me that my sons might be enemies for life," confided one mother. "In private, my husband and I refer to them as 'Cain and Abel.' It's a joke, but not a very funny one." Like this mother, many parents fear the worst when they witness the rivalry that is, in fact, a normal dynamic. Much of the bickering and one-upmanship we observe among siblings can be attributed to their very natural desires—to express uniqueness, to get a better deal from a parent, to be the best loved, to avoid sharing, to carve out a special space, or to gain approval. One or more of these is at work when our child tries to get us to take his or her side against a sibling. Does this dialogue sound familiar?

At the breakfast table, Rachel, nine, decides to share her worldly knowledge with her younger sister, six-year-old Beth.

RACHEL: Beth, it's not Alison Wonderland. It's Alice *in* Wonderland.

BETH: I can say it any way I want. Alison Wonderland, Alison Wonderland.

RACHEL: You're such a baby.

BETH (whining): No I'm not!

RACHEL: Oh, shut up.

BETH (whining louder): Mom! Rachel said shut up to me.

RACHEL: You're a tattletale.

BETH: Mommee!

RACHEL: Tattletale. Baby.

BETH: Meanie! Stinko!

MOM (firmly): There's no name calling in this house.

RACHEL: Well, she's such a baby.

BETH: I am not.

MOM: There is to be no name calling.

RACHEL: Well, I can if I want to.

MOM: No. I can't stop you from getting mad at each other, but in this house people are not to be called names. That's the rule.

This mother handled the situation with remarkable calm, keeping herself from getting embroiled in the squabble. She was realistic enough to know that children will fight no matter what and that their arguing is inevitable. However, *she did not take sides.* She firmly stated the rule—"no name calling"—without blaming either child. More frequently, parents are unwittingly drawn into the squabble, yelling "Leave your sister alone" . . . "Act your age—you're older, you should know better" . . . "Stop being mean—your sister didn't do anything to hurt you" . . . "Who started it this time?"

It's a fact of life: Children will naturally seek to gain the upper hand in a family, often at the expense of a younger or more vulnerable sibling. They will observe one another closely and take advantage of any edge they can achieve.

I can remember it happening when I was young. I was the second child, and I played the role of being the "good girl," because my brother was always acting up—refusing to eat his dinner, sneaking out of bed at night, not doing his homework. My brother resented me for acting like a goody-goody and for being a tattletale and trying to get him into trouble whenever I could. As a result, he behaved in a very physical way with me. He used to take my arm and bend it behind my back or shove me down and sit on me. When we played ball, it was usually thrown hard at my head. I resented and feared him, especially when he was angry at me, which he often was, because I was more subdued and tried to please our parents, especially when he was being naughty and aggressive. And looking back, I can now see that I deserved his resentment. I was not an innocent party. In my sly little way, I used to drive him crazy. We were both guilty—I of deliberately pushing his buttons, and he of reacting with force. Today, as is the case with most siblings once they grow up, we get along very well.

Parents also complain that morning crises are exacerbated by sibling fights. "It's like a seesaw," observed Sarah, one of my students, who is the mother of a six-year-old boy and a four-year-old girl. "Sometimes it feels as though Blaine and Jody have planned it so that one of them is always being obnoxious. Our mornings are like a time bomb with a different fuse every day. Some mornings Jody is fine, and Blaine will start trouble; some mornings it's the other way around."

MOM (to Jody): Come on, sweetheart, you have to get up now.

JODY: No!

MOM (angrily): Jody, let's go! [I go into the kitchen, already uptight, and pour cereal, milk, and juice for Blaine, who is acting sweet and agreeable.]

BLAINE: Thank you, Mommy.

MOM: You're welcome, sweetheart. [Then I go into the bathroom to take a quick shower. Still not dressed, Jody comes in whining as I'm shampooing my hair. Then off she goes to the kitchen to begin World War III with her favorite enemy. As I'm rinsing off, I hear . . .]

BLAINE: Stop it! I'm watching GI Joe.

JODY: No, I want to watch Jem.

BLAINE: Mommy, Jody's bothering me!

JODY: No, I'm not.

MOM (dripping from the shower and feeling her blood pressure rise): You kids stop it out there!

BLAINE (loudly): I have more Cheerios than you, and yours are soggy. Ha! Ha!

JODY (crying): I want new cereal.

BLAINE: Corey's coming over today to play Nintendo, and you can't play.

JODY: *Mommy!* Blaine's being mean to me!

MOM (storming into the kitchen): That's it! You kids are driving me crazy. Blaine, no friends after school today. And no dessert tonight for either of you. And no more TV in the morning if you're going to fight. . . . [And so on with the threats.]

Sarah's complaint "You kids are driving me crazy!" gets at the heart of the way most parents feel when their kids fight. We believe that our children are in league together against us—and, indeed, this is sometimes true. Subtle teamwork is designed to get a parent's goat. Seeing Mom or Dad explode can relieve boredom, put off the inevitable daily chores, or interrupt a parent who is having a rare moment of peace. (Parents often report that as soon as they get on the phone, the fights begin.) Sometimes children fight as a way of getting attention, and to try to get an adult to take their side against the other. Sarah felt that what she called the "morning wars" between Jody and Blaine really *were* driving her crazy. "I try to stay out of the middle, but the fights escalate until I have to step in," she said. "And by that time, I'm yelling." What can Sarah do? Hard as it is, she might try staying out of it and refusing to arbitrate. She can say "You kids work it out. I'm busy getting ready for work." After a few mornings, they might get the idea that Mom isn't going to get involved, and then they might decide that it's boring to fight if there's no adult around to intercede.

The Myth of Loving Siblings

I have sometimes used an exercise for parents in my classes who are concerned with sibling rivalry. I ask, "How many of you are siblings?" Most people raise their hands. Then I go to the blackboard and ask them to call out words that recall the feelings they had for their brothers and sisters when they were children.

Hate
Disgust
Envy
Wishing they'd never been born
Rage
Resentment
Embarrassment
Fear
Loathing
Fury

Impatience
Competitiveness

Occasionally, they also mention admiration for older
siblings who were their idols. They recall positive feelings
as well, especially loyalty, or protectiveness by an older
child for a younger child, but these feelings are recalled
with less frequency. After the list is completed, I ask them
to recall specific things they said to their siblings and that
their siblings said to them.

You're a baby.
You're stupid.
You can't play.
You're always bad.
This is mine, and you can't have any.
You're doggy doodoo.
You're ugly.
Four-eyes!
You're a fatso.
Nobody likes you.
Crybaby!
Teacher's pet.

Laughing, they also provide a lengthy list of "gross epithets," including pimplepuss, shit-for-brains, fart-face,
shithead, penis-breath, and others. My students seem to
enjoy this exercise, and their lists are always long and colorful. Then I ask them to give me words that describe their
hopes for the way their children will relate to one another.
I write their responses on the other side of the blackboard.

Loving
Happy together

Sharing
Watching out for one another
Having fun and cooperating
Loyal
Protective
Best friends
Affectionate
Caring for or teaching younger siblings

Everyone immediately notices the dramatic contrast between the two sides of the blackboard. "Can you see how your memories of your own experiences clash with your expectations for your children?" I ask. They nod in recognition. When parents see the enormous gap between their idealistic expectations and the everyday reality, it helps them be more accepting of the sibling battles. It also reminds them that as children grow up and reach adulthood, the hostility and competition usually lessen, and are gradually replaced by closeness and support.

The reality of sibling behavior is in direct opposition to all of our fantasies about having a "happy" family—one that is peaceful and harmonious. In spite of what we may have experienced in our own childhoods, we cling to a vision (established by television sitcoms like "Leave It to Beaver") of loving children who are kind to each other and rarely fight. When our own children don't fit the ideal, we blame them for creating negative friction in what we believe should be a conflict-free household. Parents are eager to learn the skills that will end the battles, but before they can learn skills, they must first revise their expectations.

It's useful to remember that children can't help feeling as they do, and many well-intentioned parents try to minimize or deny a child's feelings because they hear them as cruel or unloving. But when a child is upset with a sibling, he or she needs a parent to respond by acknowledging those feelings, not by saying, for example, "How could you feel so mean toward your little brother? He's such a sweet baby."

Parents need to accept the feelings of jealousy, resentment, or anger that a sibling might have, while setting limits on hurtful actions. A parent might say "It's hard to have to share Mommy." Or "Sometimes you wish you could have Daddy to yourself." Or "Sometimes Jeffrey gets you very annoyed. I know. But he's not to be hit."

It's also helpful to know when to intervene and when to leave children alone to settle their own disputes. In *The Sibling Bond,* Stephen Bank and Michael Kahn write: "Some parents station themselves, like Solomon the Wise, at the center of their children's conflicts, continually setting themselves up as a source of mediation." But the authors warn: "Because conflict is a major language of normal sibling relationships, parental interference—ill-timed, overreactive, overinvolved, all-wise—can undercut the problem-solving capacities of children and adolescents."

Penelope, the mother of twin eight-year-old girls, complained that her daughters were constantly squabbling and running from her to her husband to gain support. "If I won't listen to them, they'll find their father, and he'll intervene by punishing them both in a way that I don't like. Or he'll hear them fighting and run in to quiet them down and stop the argument. There's a lot of tension as a result of this, not only between my girls, but also among the four of us."

I suggested to Penelope that she enlist her husband's support. "Ask him if he'd be willing to cooperate with an experiment you might want to try. When the girls fight, why not try to leave them alone to resolve their own dispute, instead of running in to find out who's at fault or who started it, and acting as a referee." She agreed and at the next class, she reported this incident.

"Monday afternoon, after school, we heard shouting coming from the girls' room. Then Elyse ran into the living room, and Mara followed close behind.

" 'She kicked me!' screamed Elyse.

" 'She punched me first,' yelled Mara.

"Then they were at each other, shouting 'I did not,' 'You did too,' and so on. My husband calmly viewed this scene from his position on the sofa. The girls tried to get him involved, but he just said, 'I'm sure you two can settle this yourselves.'

"They ran into the kitchen to see if they could enlist my help, but I said, 'I'm sorry you're not getting along right now, but I'm sure you can work it out.'

"They stopped and stared at me. What was going on here? First Daddy, then me. They turned around and quietly (probably because they were shocked) walked back into their room."

Leona, another student, spoke of how angry she got when she saw her two children being hostile toward each other. "Jennifer teases Paul a lot—she's two years older. She hits him or pulls his hair. So I say, 'No pulling hair.' But sometimes he hits her back and pulls her hair, then it turns into a free-for-all, and I can't stop it."

"Perhaps you could try using a timer," I suggested to Leona. Say 'I'm going to separate you until the timer rings. I can't leave you in the same room now. It's not safe.' Try it. Often, as soon as you separate them, they can't wait to be together."

One issue that comes up a lot is the anger children feel when they lose their "favored place" with the arrival of a new baby. Although we need to love all of our children, we also have to accept the fact that they are not always going to love each other. The new baby doesn't seem like such a bundle of joy to an envious sibling. He didn't choose to share our affection. Anna Quindlen, a *New York Times* columnist, observed with typical humor and insight her three-year-old's growing realization that the new addition to their family was there to stay: "It began one day when the younger one needed me more and I turned to my older son, Quin, and said, 'You know, Quin, I'm Christopher's mommy too.' The look that passed over his face was the one that usually accompanies the discovery of a dead body in the den: shock, denial, horror. 'And Daddy is Christopher's daddy too?' he gasped. When I confirmed this, he began to cry—wet, sad, sobbing."

Writer Judith Viorst expressed well the underlying confusion and jealousy in the poem "Some Things Don't Make Any Sense at All," in *If I Were in Charge of the World and Other Worries* (New York: Atheneum, 1981):

My mom says I'm her sugarplum
My mom says I'm her lamb.
My mom says I'm completely perfect
Just the way I am.
My mom says I'm her super-special,
Wonderful, terrific little guy.
My mom just had another baby.
Why?

Children Hurting Children

Frequently in my classes, the subject comes up of what to do when older children behave in aggressively physical ways toward younger children.

"It's a familiar scene in our house," groaned a mother in my workshop. "I'll go into the living room because there's screaming, and I'll find my older son, Rick, who is ten, wrestling on the floor with Mason, who is only six. I'll start yelling for Rick to stop it, he's hurting Mason. But some-times Rick will say 'I'm not hurting him. He likes it.' And it's true that Mason appears to be undamaged. But I'm not sure about this. It upsets me to see a bigger one being too physical with the smaller one. I don't want my child to be a bully."

When we see our children being physically violent with one another, it can make us enraged. Ironically, the first tendency is often to react violently ourselves. I saw this expressed very well in a cartoon that showed a boy being held over his father's knee; as the father spanked him, he said, "This will teach you to hit your baby brother!" Hitting a child to teach him not to hit is a futile strategy, since our children learn most from watching our behavior. But many parents have admitted to me that when they see their children hitting and hurting each other, that's when they come closest to reacting themselves by hitting and hurting. It's a common dilemma. What can they do?

I think it is important that parents learn to acknowledge a child's aggressive, negative feelings without giving the child permission to act them out physically. One parent found a way, as she related in this confrontation that oc-curred between her two children.

"I was in the kitchen at six-thirty one evening—a bad time for me always—with my sons, three years old and twenty-one months. Jake, the three-year-old, hit his little brother, knocking him down. I felt so angry I wanted to hit Jake and show him how it feels. Instead, I clenched my teeth to control myself, stooped down, and held his arms. I said, 'Jake, I am so angry that you knocked Jon over that I want to hit you.' He started to cry, and I went on, still holding his arms. 'But I am not going to, because hitting would hurt you. That's why I clenched my teeth and made that face—to stop myself. You must learn when you want to hit to do something to stop yourself, too.' He stopped crying and began to get calmer. When I had his full attention, I talked to him about using words instead of shoving or hitting. We also talked about getting a punching bag so he could have something to hit."

Sometimes it's helpful to indulge your children's fantasies about a sibling. Everyone has fantasies—like the mother who imagined putting her daughter up for adoption at the supermarket or the three-year-old who wanted to put the new baby in the oven. Fantasies are okay, but acting them out is not okay. You might say to a child who is speaking resentfully of the new baby or saying she wished the baby would go back to the hospital "You wish you could have Mommy and Daddy all to yourself. You don't like it when the baby cries. You don't like it when Mommy takes time with the baby. I know. But no hitting." It's better than screaming "Leave him alone! What's the matter with you? What are you trying to do—kill him?" Or "In this house, there is only love"—which leaves the child confused and resentful, since she *isn't* feeling love at that moment.

The Fairness Trap

Children can find bottomless reserves of righteousness, moral indignation, and resentment—when the object is another child. When I was a child, part of the role I carved out for myself of being the "good girl" was to be the official reporter of all my brother's bad behavior. If we were not allowed to jump on the bed, and he jumped on the bed, my mother would know about it within seconds. If I caught my brother playing when he was supposed to be doing homework, I would report it immediately. No wonder when he wasn't hitting me, my brother was busy hiding from me.

My mother finally put a stop to my tattling by telling us that whoever tattled would get punished.

Children also have antennae poised to catch the smallest inequality. They complain constantly that "It's not fair," equating fairness with sameness. They will watch you like hawks to be sure they're receiving their fair share—right down to the last crumb of a cookie or the duration of a hug. One mother related the story of what happened when her five-year-old twins, Joy and Jess, were each given a goldfish at the school fair. "A week later, I found Jess sobbing because her goldfish had died. I was sympathetic. I put my arms around her and said, 'No wonder you're sad. You were getting so attached to Goldie, and now he's dead.' She looked tearfully up at me and said emphatically, 'That isn't why I'm crying. I'm crying because my goldfish died, and Joy's didn't!' " Ironically, although children clamor for special position, they are often obsessed with being treated exactly the same. One parent, Margaret, shared this dialogue, which focuses on an all-too-familiar fairness issue.

Margaret gave each of her sons one of their favorite treats, a Hostess cupcake.

ZEKE: How many are left?

MARGARET: There are two left. You can each have one today and one tomorrow.

ZEKE: Jesse doesn't get any more.

MARGARET: Why not?

ZEKE: Because he got one yesterday, and I didn't.

MARGARET: Yesterday is history. You can each have one today and one tomorrow.

ZEKE: Then Jesse will have gotten an extra!

MARGARET: Stop keeping score!

ZEKE (whining): But it's not fair.

MARGARET: You're the only one who cares. Jesse doesn't

care. Last week when we bought penny candy, your bag was bigger than his, and he didn't complain.

ZEKE: He didn't know.

MARGARET: Maybe so. But he got what he wanted, so he was happy.

Margaret admitted to being frustrated by this incident. She couldn't stand it when her children kept score, and it was something Zeke in particular did a lot. She also acknowledged that she often reinforced the "fairness trap" by trying to make everything equal.

Not only is it always impossible to give each child exactly the same treatment, trying to do so robs them of their individuality. To the extent it can be managed, parents can try to focus on the uniqueness of each child, as a way of helping siblings be less jealous of one another. Trina, the mother of a two-year-old boy and a six-year-old girl, presented the following dialogue in a workshop, as an example of how subjective the matter of equal treatment can be. She had been playing with her two-year-old, tickling him and making him laugh, when Amy came into the room and demanded equal treatment.

AMY: Will you tickle me like you just tickled Sammy?

TRINA: Yes—once you get in your bed, I'll tickle you.

AMY: Okay. [She gets in bed, and Trina tickles her.]

AMY (starting to cry): That's not how you did it with Sammy.

TRINA: Yes, it is. I tickled his belly, and he fell into the pillows, just like you.

AMY: It was different.

TRINA: You are you, and Sammy is Sammy. He laughed a

lot, but you didn't think it tickled. Tomorrow, before
you go to sleep, I'll tickle you again.

AMY: That's not fair.

After Trina read her dialogue in class, she was the first
to admit that it was an example of the fairness issue reaching
a new height of absurdity. "I don't want to have to watch
every twitch and nuance to be sure they're exactly the
same," she said. "And I don't want to treat my children
like they're clones."

Trina handled the situation well, but she was frustrated
that Amy still felt she was being treated unfairly. Parents
have to accept the fact that children won't always perceive
their actions as being fair. It's best not to dwell on it too
much. "It's not fair" is the refrain of siblings. Trina could
have responded by giving Amy a hug and acknowledging
her complaint by saying "It doesn't seem fair to you. I
know."

Meryl found that when her son Robert, eight, was in a
grumpy mood, which happened most often in the mornings,
he tended to focus on the inequities between the way she
treated him and his six-year-old brother, William. "Since
William is younger, he needs more attention in the morning," said Meryl. "I think Robert understands this, but he
insists on making all of our mornings miserable by whining.
Every morning, I wake up feeling good, and want to avoid
morning confrontations so my children can go off to school
in a happy mood. But the mornings rarely end up being
pleasant, and I feel guilty about that. Yet, I don't like having
to walk on eggshells wondering how best to handle Robert."
When I asked her for an example, Meryl supplied this
dialogue of a typical "bad start" morning.

MERYL: Robert and William, time to get up!

ROBERT: You turned the light on, and I wasn't ready.

MERYL: Well, Robert, I had to see. Cover your eyes until you're ready. [Walks away from Robert's bed, over to William's bed.]

ROBERT: You love William more than you love me!

MERYL: Robert, you know that's not true. If anything happened to either of you, my heart would be broken.

ROBERT: No! You love him better. You help him dress, but you don't help me.

MERYL: Robert, you are eight years old. I'm not going to help an eight-year-old dress. That's crazy. Now, no one wants to be around a crabby person, so you come downstairs with a smile on your face.

"By this point," admitted Meryl, "the day has started all wrong. And that example is mild. Sometimes Robert's whining about his brother gets me so mad I start yelling at him and telling him off. Then he feels hurt and says something like 'See? I told you you don't care about me.' Then I'll have to apologize to get things back on track. It's a mess."

Meryl felt completely stymied by the way Robert challenged her love for his brother. Since his complaints were so irrational and ill-founded, she felt poorly equipped to handle them. I reminded her that the real issue was not her love for Robert, but rather a very practical problem: how to get up and get going in the morning. I suggested she concentrate on ways to shift the focus away from a peer struggle. Several weeks later, Meryl returned with this report.

"The next time Robert woke up in a crabby mood, I put out his clothes and left the room. I didn't get involved in an argument. I said, 'As soon as you're in a better frame of mind, we can talk,' and then I went downstairs to fix breakfast. I felt much better, and when Robert came downstairs, he actually apologized to me."

I was impressed with Meryl's practical way of handling Robert's complaint, since it never works to try to convince children that we love them both the same by *telling* them. Perhaps it's because they each want to be loved the *most*, not the same at all.

Trouble With Peers

Rivalry exists, not only among siblings, but among groups of children as well. Many parents talk about how upsetting it is to see the cruelty that seems inherent in the interaction of children.

Polly, a mother in my group, described how furious she became when her daughter came home crying because a certain group of girls would not include her. "A group is formed on the basis of excluding certain people," Polly said. "And when your child is one of those who is being excluded, it can make your blood boil. In the case of my daughter, my immediate reaction was to feel enraged at these children for hurting her."

Polly wanted her daughter, Emily, to be accepted by the other girls and to feel good about herself. And she wanted to communicate that she was on her daughter's side. But she felt it would be harmful on several levels for her to get too engaged in her daughter's problem. "This was a normal problem among children," she said, "and Emily had to resolve it for herself. But I figured a little empathy was warranted. I made her a nice snack, and we sat at the kitchen table."

MOM: I guess it hurt your feelings when the girls went skating and didn't ask you.

EMILY: I hate them. They're so mean. I hope they all break their legs.

MOM: Sometimes people do things that hurt other people, even when they don't mean to.

EMILY: Someone should stop them. It's not nice.

MOM: I can see you're pretty angry about this.

EMILY (crying): Nobody likes me.

MOM (in mock horror): *Nobody?*

EMILY: Well, maybe one or two people . . .

MOM: Mmmmm . . .

EMILY: Yeah. I don't really hate those girls. I just wish they were nicer.

MOM: I remember when I was in third grade, and these girls wouldn't let me join their club. It really hurt! So I can see why you feel bad. That's the way it goes sometimes.

EMILY: It stinks.

MOM: Listen, I have to drive downtown this afternoon. Would you like to come with me?

EMILY (jumping up from the table): No, that's okay. I'm going to call Jeri and see if she wants to ride bikes.

Polly allowed Emily to vent her feelings without falling into one of the most common parent traps—that is, openly attacking the girls who treated her daughter badly or implying to Emily that she had done something to cause the reaction. Sometimes without meaning to, parents reinforce their children's pain by getting too involved and suggesting reasons why they might be having trouble making friends. This is a classic case of blaming the victim: "You should try harder" or "Maybe you're not being nice to them." Some parents will try to force the issue. Polly might have said, for example, "Surely some people like you. Why don't you

call so-and-so? Maybe she'll play with you." This reaction
would have put Emily on the spot to prove that she had
friends, or it might have convinced her that she was a
disappointment to her mother because she was not more
popular or part of the "in" group. Polly kept an appropriate
distance while offering support. What Emily really needed
was to spill out her feelings to a listening, nonjudgmental
ear. By the time she had done this, Emily had recovered
enough to seek out another friend for play.

In workshops I have conducted for teachers, I have
learned many skills. Teachers deal daily with angry and
disruptive flare-ups that occur among children, and many
of them have learned skills to help children in their peer
relationships, without taking sides. I liked the way Ellen,
a preschool teacher, handled this situation.

MARK (running up to her on the playground): Chris says
    that I'm a baby and that I wet my bed.
ELLEN: You don't like it when Chris calls you names.
MARK: No. I'm not a baby, and I don't wet my bed.
ELLEN: What do you think you could say to Chris?
MARK: I'll tell him I'm not a baby.

Ellen reported that Mark marched off to repeat those
words to Chris, and the two of them continued playing. In
the following weeks, she noticed that Mark ran to her less
frequently with complaints, and once she overheard him
telling Chris "I don't like it when you call me names. I
won't be your friend if you do that." Observed Ellen, "Mark
needed me to acknowledge his feelings and to help him
think through his actions without losing his best friend. I
find that allowing children to solve their own problems,
with me as a mediator, helps them to feel in control and
good about their actions. When I act as a nonjudgmental

sounding board, the kids often feel good about solving their own problems."

In every group of children, there are those who stand out as what I would call the charismatic leaders of the class or playground. These kids hold tremendous power and can make others miserable with nothing more than a disdainful look or a harsh word. We all knew them in our childhood, and our children have to contend with them too. A teacher in my workshop described how she handled a situation with one of the class leaders who exerted a lot of power over his less assertive classmates.

Eric came over to his teacher very upset.

ERIC: Miss Porter, Trevor said that I'm fat.

TEACHER: I understand how this would upset you, but you aren't going to let his untrue statements get you down, are you?

ERIC: He also said that my father is stupid.

TEACHER: It sounds like he was trying to make you angry. In my eyes, you are a very nice-looking young man, and having met your dad, I know that he is smart. You can tell Trevor what I said if you want to.

Eric went over and talked to Trevor. Later, the teacher took Trevor aside.

TEACHER: I've heard complaints from your friends that you have made them unhappy lately.

TREVOR (smiling boldly): I know. I like to do that.

TEACHER: I may not agree with your teasing others, but I still think you're a great kid. However, the other kids will resent you, and I really hate to see your friends dislike you. I'd like to see you make a lot of friends and be happy.

TREVOR (sheepishly): Yeah . . .
TEACHER (with a big smile): I have confidence in you, Trevor.

Some parents report that their angriest moments happen when their children are with their friends. "I'm sure Ian's friends think I'm a witch, because I'm always yelling whenever they come over to play," said one mother. "But Ian gets crazy when he's around his friends. He's wild, noisy, and disrespectful of me. I usually end up getting mad. For example, one day last week, Ian had friends over, and I took them out for pizza. In the restaurant, Ian started showing off and being sassy to me. I could tell he was trying to impress his friends with this daring behavior. I didn't say anything to him then, just gave him a look. But later, when we were alone in the car, after we had dropped his friends off, I blew up. They had been wild in the car, and I had a splitting headache. I started yelling at Ian, then he got mad. When we got home, he got out of the car and slammed the door, yelling 'You're stupid!' I followed him in the house screaming, and he screamed back, sarcastically—which I hate. 'Okay, Mom, from now on, I'll never have any fun. I'll never laugh. Would that make you happy?' "

We talked about what Ian's mother could have done or might do the next time she found herself in this situation. I suggested that she might have tried to wait a little longer, until she had calmed down, and then had a talk with Ian along these lines: "Ian, I know it's fun when you're with your friends to pretend you don't have to listen to your mother, but your rudeness is totally unacceptable. How do you think I felt when you made fun of me in front of your friends? You know I would not say embarrassing things about you in front of your friends." Later, alone with his mother,

Ian might have been receptive to hearing this, but it's not the kind of discussion that's possible in the midst of a rage.

Compassionate Intervention

Even though it is often advisable to take a back seat to our children's peer and sibling dilemmas, sometimes they need our help to find appropriate responses. Rhoda, a mother who had been in my workshop for a long time, told of this conversation she had with her ten-year-old daughter, Peggy. Peggy had just come home from a sleepover.

PEGGY: There's something I need to tell you about the sleepover. It's really bothering me.

RHODA: Do you want to talk now?

PEGGY: No, not right now.

RHODA: Okay, let me know when you're ready. You won't forget, will you?

PEGGY: No.

[Later.]

PEGGY: I need to talk now.

RHODA: Okay.

PEGGY: I'm so ashamed and embarrassed. Don't tell anyone! I think I really hurt Joey's feelings. [Joey is her friend's younger brother.] Last night when we were all having dessert, I said—it just came out—"Whoever hates Joey's guts, raise your hand." Right away, I was sorry I said it, but hardly anyone heard me. But then this girl sitting next to me said, "She said, whoever hates Joey, raise your hand." Then a lot of kids raised their hands. There. I said it. I feel better.

RHODA (feeling horrified, but trying to contain herself and not criticize): You must have been so embarrassed. And poor Joey!

PEGGY: I felt so horrible I couldn't even talk. I hope Joey has forgotten about it by now.

RHODA: Would you?

PEGGY: It's over. He's probably not even thinking about it.

RHODA: Maybe. But you are.

PEGGY: I'm never going over to Jane's house again. I'll wait a year.

RHODA: Sounds like it isn't forgotten, though. I've got to leave now, but you can think about some choices you have about what you can do—like call Joey, write him a note, or whatever.

PEGGY: Mom, it's over!

RHODA: Think about what I said.

[The next evening.]

RHODA: We have to talk about this Joey thing.

PEGGY: See. I knew I shouldn't have told you.

RHODA: Honey, I can see why you'd like to drop it, but this is a matter that needs to be talked about. It seems to me you have a choice. You can be very uncomfortable about what happened and do nothing about it, try to avoid it, and keep the uncomfortable feelings. Or you can call Joey or his mom, explain or apologize, and feel totally relieved.

PEGGY: I can't call Joey.

RHODA: Then call his mother, and she'll tell him. Do you want me to get her on the phone, and then you can talk to her?

PEGGY (panicking): No! Uh . . . okay. [Rhoda dialed the number and said hello to Jane's mother, then handed the phone to Peggy.]

PEGGY (trembling and nervous): Hi . . . I'm calling because I feel so awful about what I said to Joey. I thought it was a joke—but it wasn't. Okay . . . bye. [She hangs up the phone.] She said it took a lot of courage to call.

RHODA: She was right! You must have a great feeling of relief. Now it's *really* over. I'll bet you're proud of yourself. You did something that even grown-ups would find difficult.

This is an example of a skillful mother who gently taught her daughter a lesson about kindness and values, without lecturing. It would have been tempting but unhelpful for Rhoda to say "That's terrible" (Peggy already knew that) or "You should be ashamed" (she already was). What Peggy needed was nonjudgmental guidance, and that's what Rhoda gave her.

Children are often reluctant to confide in parents about what goes on between them and their peers, and parents are usually dying to know as many details as possible. "I trust my child," one father explained, "but it's a big, bad world out there. Our kids are exposed to drugs and violence and the kinds of pressure that we never had to deal with when we were kids." He was rightfully concerned, but I believe that the solution is not to impose tight control but rather to emphasize useful guidelines. In her excellent book *Too Smart for Trouble*, Sharon Scott lists some good ways for kids, five to ten years old, to avoid negative peer pressure. Parents who have concerns about their children's ability to cope with peer pressure might do well to refer to Scott's book. In it, she supplies a number of practical and effective options—both words and actions—that children can use to sidestep pressure to do things that might get them into trouble.

We can be effective guides in helping our children maneuver the delicate roads of peer relationships—whether with siblings or with friends. Although they live in a world we cannot completely inhabit, we can be there to provide a steady hand along the way. We can't solve their problems when they fight with a sibling or are upset by an encounter with a peer. But we can help them to become good decision makers and problem solvers for themselves.

5

Going It Alone

If parents are going to divorce and not scar their children for
life, they should keep them out of what's going on . . . they
shouldn't make them suffer . . . or try to make them hate the
other parent.   —a fifteen-year-old child of divorce
                   from *How It Feels When Parents Divorce*,
                   by Jill Krementz

Nancy and her ex-husband, Pierre, have been divorced for seven years. It was a bitter parting, since
Nancy did not want the divorce, and Pierre did.
Nancy has adjusted well—although it took her several years
to accept the idea that her marriage was over—but she
complains that Pierre's attitude has made it difficult if not
impossible to let go of her anger. "I am willing to put aside
my own feelings for the sake of our son, Ronnie, who is
eleven. But Pierre won't speak to me at all. He makes plans
with Ronnie independently, without telling me. I never
know from one minute to the next what those plans are.
I have to force them out of Ronnie, and if they interfere
with my plans, no one seems to care. Lately, I've found
myself being angry at Ronnie about this, which I know isn't
right. He's clearly in the middle. I decided I had to have

an honest talk with my son and try to deal with the situation directly."

NANCY: Ronnie, I need to set some ground rules for us about visitation with your father.

RONNIE: What? I told you Dad is picking me up Friday, and I'm staying with him this weekend.

NANCY: I know you told me this morning. But Thursday morning is late to be hearing it for the first time. Look, I am running a house, managing a business, and having to organize both our schedules. All I'm asking is that you respect the fact that we live together and I have to take care of you. Making plans without checking with me first is not showing respect for the fact that I too have things I need to take care of.

RONNIE: Okay . . . okay . . .

"I could tell he was tuning me out," said Nancy. "I admit I felt a little sorry for him. It's uncomfortable for him, but since his father won't speak with me directly, there's nothing else I can do about it. I hate putting Ronnie in the middle. It seems unfair."

Nancy's complaint is just one in a long series of distressing stories I hear from the single parents (mostly mothers) who attend my workshops. Listening to them, I marvel at their ability to cope at all. Their lives seem to be filled with mixed signals, broken commitments, heated arguments, and hostile children, and the mothers are often blamed by their children for problems over which they have no control. They speak with great passion—and often fury—about how hard it is to keep all the pieces together, especially since they are often carrying most if not all the burden of raising their children.

Recently, I gathered together a group of single mothers to focus more specifically on the issues they face—and how they cope with their anger. To hear these mothers tell it, one would never guess that an emancipation of women had occurred in our times. All of the women were the primary caretakers for their children. Even in joint-custody arrangements, the women reported that they still performed all the essential functions of shopping for clothes, arranging doctor appointments, getting children haircuts, and the like. When emergency calls were made from school, it was almost never the father who left work to pick up the child. The joint custody was not entirely "joint" and certainly not equal.

I (who would have been overwhelmed at having to raise my children alone) was impressed with how the mothers handled their lives and the enormous strength and responsibility they brought to their child rearing. Yet their stories brought home in a very real way the sad compromises people are often forced to make—and how far from the ideal the reality of family life can be.

Shattered Ideals

When we enter into marriage, we are conscious of making a commitment that has been blessed throughout history as natural and right. We move away from our birth families and enter into the exciting adventure of creating families of our own. In this pursuit, we are buttressed by the power of our traditions and the positive reinforcement of a society in which many consider marriage and family the highest ideal.

Divorce shatters that. It is a cruel intrusion on a family's dreams for the future that can leave everyone involved with a feeling of hanging in the air without a net. Divorce is never easy. It's full of pain, loss, and a sense of failure or abandonment. It's a fate no one would choose, given better options—and children are at the center of the storm. As Linda Bird Francke observes in *Growing Up Divorced,* "Begotten and born most often in love, children are living proof after divorce of love gone wrong, consistent reminders of the broken promises of marriage." This is a heavy burden for kids to carry, and sometimes divorcing parents, caught up in their own grief, forget that their children are suffering too. Writes Francke:

> The child's world turns topsy-turvy. Not only does he lose one parent from the household; he often loses both when the remaining parent has to go to work. He may have to move, change schools, cope with the new responsibilities and demands of a single-parent home, adjust to seeing the departed parent part-time or even not at all. In the long run, divorce invariably breeds financial complications, loyalty conflicts, pressure on the child to maintain close ties with both parents, and the strain of sorting out relationships in a stepfamily.

Our ideals about the way families *should* be leave little room for a single parent bearing the burden of child raising alone, or the chaotic systems of shuttling children back and forth between two homes. Even when divorce is considered a positive, mutually agreed-upon choice, the sense of rejection by society and of not fitting in can be hard to overcome. Patricia, a woman in her thirties who had been divorced for two years, articulated the sentiments of many when she described her struggle to feel like a "whole" family unit with her twin five-year-old sons. "It's not an automatic transition," she said, "even when it's for the best, which it definitely was in our case. I often feel envious when I watch so-called intact families and wish mine were like that." She laughed. "I'm over my husband, but I'm not over wanting the ideal of what family should be. I feel that something is missing, and the feeling gets reinforced whenever I take the boys somewhere. In restaurants, the waiters ask 'Are there *only* three?' At movie theaters, '*Only* three?' Last week we went on a trip to visit their grandparents. At the airport, the ticket agent asked, '*Only* three?' It's as though everyone is trying to remind us that we're incomplete."

Children are caught in the middle during a divorce, and they usually have little understanding of the vague "adult" calamities that have driven their parents apart. They require a special dose of compassion and extra attention during this period, but often parents who are themselves physically exhausted and emotionally wounded find it hard to give.

The women who participated in my group talked openly about these dilemmas, and how they've worked to restore stability in their own lives and the lives of their children.

The Guilty Party

"I forced the separation and divorce," Patricia said. "My sons adore their father. They don't see the side of him that is careless and irresponsible—he's an alcoholic. They only know that I made him leave, and sometimes I know they blame me. They ask 'Why can't Daddy live here?' or cry 'I miss Daddy.' It's so hard to watch them on the days they come home from a visit. They're so sad, and I want to help them, but I don't know how."

Laura, whose daughter is four, related this conversation that occurred shortly after she and her husband separated.

DEBBIE: Why can't Daddy stay here? Why?

LAURA: Honey, your father and I decided we'd be happier apart. But we both love you just as much.

DEBBIE: If Daddy loved me, he wouldn't leave. Why did you make him leave! [Crying.]

LAURA: I didn't make him. We decided—

DEBBIE: You did! You did! You're mean. I heard you yelling.

LAURA: I lost my temper, because I was mad. But that's not why Daddy is living in a separate apartment.

DEBBIE: I miss him. I wish we weren't divorced.

LAURA: Me, too, honey. But sometimes things happen that make us sad. Don't worry, though. Daddy is coming tomorrow to take you for two whole days—just the two of you. Maybe you can tell him how you feel.

DEBBIE: I will!

After this encounter, even though Laura had treated her daughter's sadness and anger with sensitivity and respect, she felt depressed and very guilty. She began to question whether she and her husband had been selfish in deciding to part. "We did it because we thought it would make *us* happier, but it didn't make Debbie happier. It felt like two adults ganging up to wreck a little girl's life. I told myself that the hurt would pass, but I couldn't be sure that Debbie would not be damaged somehow by this. To make matters worse, her father was three hours late picking her up, and I had to comfort her all over again when it looked like he might not show up."

The prospect of divorce is frightening to children, because they don't understand what will happen to them. But they don't always respond to the news with tears and anger that can be addressed directly. Kathleen and Wayne found out, after the fact, that their seven-year-old son had deep fears he was afraid to share.

"We had a fairly amicable divorce," Kathleen said. "There wasn't a lot of screaming and carrying on, so it came as a surprise to our son, Barry. We planned to tell him on the actual day Wayne was moving to a new apartment. We decided we would sit down with Barry and have a talk, then he could accompany his father to the apartment and see for himself that it was okay and that he would have a room there. We sat down with him. Wayne said, 'Barry, we have something very important to talk about. Your mother and I feel that we would be happier if we didn't live in the same house.' We were watching Barry's face— strangely, he didn't seem to be paying attention. He was looking around the room, not at his father or me. Wayne kept talking, and I joined in, explaining exactly what would happen, and reassuring Barry that we both loved him very much and that would not change, even if we lived in different places. He was still not reacting. In my naïveté, I actually believed he wasn't upset by the news. I thought perhaps because he had some friends whose parents were divorced, he might not find it too unsettling. Wayne and I had decided on joint custody—Wayne is a wonderful father—and so we could assure Barry that he would spend time with both of us and have his own room at Wayne's apartment.

"The day went much better than we expected. Wayne and I were both relieved that Barry took the news so well. In the following weeks, we watched him closely for any signs of trauma, but he seemed happy enough, and it was an adventure for him to go to a different apartment several days a week.

"Then, about two months after Wayne left, when I felt the worst was over, I received a call from Barry's teacher. 'Is something happening at home that I should be aware of?' she asked. My heart fell. I said yes, and told her about the divorce. She was a very compassionate woman, and she said, 'That might explain why Barry has been behaving so aggressively in the classroom.' She went on to tell me that in recent weeks our formerly gentle child had become a behavior problem—picking fights on the playground, refusing to follow instructions in class, and quarreling with his friends when he was supposed to be reading quietly. I told his teacher that I honestly hadn't observed any change in his behavior at home. We talked for a while, and she suggested that Barry might benefit from counseling with a man whose specialty it was to help children over the rough spots of divorce. 'Some of my students' parents have found him to be helpful,' she said.

"So we took Barry to this man, and after the first session, the counselor met with us. 'He's very angry about the divorce,' he told us. We were so surprised! We hadn't known it—or had been too blind to see it. The counselor suggested that Barry was afraid to voice his anger because he was worried we might leave him. It was a real moment of truth. With the counselor's advice, Wayne and I are now helping Barry talk about his anger and sadness, instead of always jumping in to reassure him. We try to acknowledge that this is a hard adjustment for all of us—Barry too."

Like adults, children can react to divorce in many different ways, and we need to listen carefully for what they are experiencing. Some common reactions are expressed in the following statements that parents have heard from their children:

Maybe since they don't love each other they might stop
    loving me.
If I stop being bad, they might get back together.
What did I do to make them get a divorce?

If I'm not good on my visits, Daddy won't want to see
me anymore.

I feel like they're always competing for me—pulling me
in opposite directions.

If he loved me, he wouldn't have left.

Nobody cares about what I want.

How could she [he/they] wreck our nice home?

People say they love you, then they leave.

I hate them.

They wish I wasn't here.

My daddy has a new family. He doesn't want me
anymore.

And so on. It is not uncommon for children to feel that
they are somehow to blame for the divorce—if only they
were better, quieter, smarter, sweeter, and more cooperative, their parents might change their minds and get
back together. Parents sometimes unwittingly reinforce
these feelings. The mother who angrily shouts "You're
just like your father!" can start the wheels spinning in
a child's head that maybe, if that's the case, she'll leave
him, too.

Sometimes divorce brings to the surface negative feelings that are hard to address. Marie and her husband,
Jack, went through a particularly grueling divorce—fighting
every step of the way. It took nearly two years for them
to reach an agreement on custody and child support. In
the aftermath of the battle, Jack freely badmouthed Marie
to their son, Jeff. Marie had tried to explain to her ex-
husband how damaging that could be, but he refused to listen. One Sunday night, Jeff came back very upset from a
weekend with his father. Marie related their conversation.

JEFF: Mommy, did you want me when I was born?

MARIE (startled): Of course, sweetheart. What a silly question.

JEFF: Dad says you didn't want to be a mother because you liked your job too much. He said you wanted an abortion.

MARIE (truly horrified and enraged with her ex-husband): You know how much I love you.

JEFF: But you didn't then.

MARIE: Jeff, you know that sometimes your dad feels angry with me, and he says things that hurt.

JEFF: I know—but just tell me the truth.

MARIE: Okay. The truth is that since the instant I felt you in my tummy, I loved you more than anything else in the world.

JEFF (somewhat appeased): Okay.

MARIE: Can I tell you a secret?

JEFF: What?

MARIE (leaning over and whispering in his ear): If you weren't in my life, my heart would be broken forever. You're my favorite person in the whole world!

JEFF (with a big smile): You're my favorite too—except for Daddy. You're both my favorite!

We have to admire how thoughtfully Marie responded to her son, in spite of her rage at her ex-husband's deliberately cruel and wounding words. It's hard to understand how in trying to hurt one's ex, the parent can use a child in such a hurtful way. But some parents find the temptation is very great to spill out some of their hostility toward a former spouse in front of the children. Or they try to win their child's favor, wanting him to see that his father (or mother) is a rotten human being. Involving a child in adult hostilities is a form of abuse. No matter how angry the parents are with one another, their children are not equipped to deal with such statements as these:

Your father is late again. That shows how much he cares!
Sure, he's fun to be with. He's trying to buy your love.
Your mother is a bitch. Now you see why I left her.
I'm the one who really takes care of you—where is he when you need new shoes or a visit to the doctor or dinner every night?
Maybe I'd be more fun and prettier too [like a father's new wife] if I didn't have to work so hard and raise you, too.
Your father didn't mail the child-support check. He doesn't care if you starve!
She's trying to control you. You don't have to pay attention to her stupid rules.
He's a drunk.
You wouldn't think he was so great if you knew what I know about him.
Who is your father [mother] seeing on weekends? Is there a girlfriend [boyfriend]?
She's spoiling you rotten.
Mom won't buy you that game? Okay, I'll do it.

The bitterness of one spouse toward another victimizes the child—and to what end? When parents divorce, no matter how deep their conflict, it is imperative that they make a pact never to badmouth each other in front of the children. Granted, this sometimes takes great self-control, but it is essential. In *Vicki Lansky's Divorce Book for Parents*, Lansky proposes that parents learn to use a new language, which she calls "divorce speak." Advises Lansky:

Watch what you say. Keep an eye on your body language. Your threats, sarcasms, and put-downs are harmful to a child already living with insecurity and fear of abandonment. These will, in the long run, damage your relationship with your child. After all, no matter how low, despicable, unthinking, lazy, abusive or cheap your ex was or is, a child will still want to love that parent. As a child matures, he or she can decide whether that love or adoration should continue without any input from you.

Everyday Conflicts

Pat had made a firm rule that her ten-year-old son, Eric, was not allowed to take the subway alone. Usually his father, who lived uptown, took the subway down to get him for the weekend, then brought him back. But one day Eric let it slip that he had taken the subway home by himself.

PAT (screaming): You took the subway *alone?*

ERIC (a little defiantly): Yes! Dad put me on the right train, and I was okay. I'm alive, aren't I?

PAT (angry and scared): Don't be smart with me, young man. You know the rules.

ERIC: Dad says you're too protective of me. *He* thinks I'm old enough. Why can't you?

PAT (growing angrier at the accusation): If you are going to do it behind my back, I won't let you visit your father overnight.

ERIC (jumping up so his chair tips over): Leave me alone! You're mean! No wonder Dad hates you. I hate you too. [Runs out of the room.]

Pat was shaken by this encounter. She sat at the table and cried for a few minutes. She knew it had been wrong for her to threaten Eric with not seeing his father. How could she have said such a thing? She wondered, feeling a deep pain inside, whether Eric really felt his father hated her—and whether he would join his father in taking sides against her. It wasn't fair. She was the one who did so much for Eric everyday. It was easy for his father to waltz in on weekends, indulge him in toys and treats, and disparage all her rules.

Another mother talked about a confrontation that developed one night when her ex-husband came to pick up their daughter. She was, she admitted, unprepared for the angry scene that erupted as a result of what she thought was an innocuous statement.

"When Stephanie's father was picking her up for the weekend, I said, 'This Thanksgiving, Stephanie will be staying here with me.' Right away, Stephanie started to scream, 'No, I'm not! I want to be with Dad. And I want to spend the Fourth of July with him too.' It made me angry, especially since she had said several times before that she wanted to spend the Fourth of July with me. I went after her and told her this behavior was not appropriate. As I turned back to go into the house, Stephanie yelled, 'Stupid!' It hurt my feelings, but I could say nothing, since she was already in the car. But when she came back at the end of the weekend, I told her how angry and hurt I was by her remarks. She had this look on her face that told me she already knew this was coming. I said, 'How else could you have handled it?' Stephanie said, 'I could have said it nice.' That night, before she went to bed, we talked more about the holidays, and Stephanie admitted, 'I love you both, and I don't want to have to choose.' "

It is very painful for parents who are devoted to the well-being of their children to realize that they feel caught in the middle, divided by our tug-of-war. Divorced parents sometimes find themselves vying for their children's love. Perhaps this is not what they intend, but it is a hard thing to avoid, especially if one parent is able to give a child more toys, nicer clothes, or a fancier house. Eve, a woman in my workshop who had been divorced for six years, told the group that she didn't know what to do about her ex-husband's habit of giving their nine-year-old daughter, Samantha, everything she wanted.

"I am on a very tight budget," she said. "I can't give Samantha all that she wants. And besides, it's not what she needs, to have every request met. But once a month, she visits her father for the weekend, and she'll tell him, 'Mom says I can't have that Barbie outfit,' or whatever, and he'll say, 'That's okay. I'll get it for you.' "

"How do you feel when you hear that?" I asked.

"It makes me angry at Samantha for asking him, and furious at her father for trying to buy her love." Eve sighed. "I'm the one who is raising her. I have the day-to-day problems to deal with, the meals to cook, the laundry to wash. He comes sweeping in once a month like a White Knight, and she is dazzled. Of course, I feel resentful."

"What do you say to Samantha when she comes home from a visit with new toys that you have refused her?"

She blushed. "I'm not especially proud of my response. I say 'Sure, he can show up once a month and give you everything your heart desires. But where is he every day?' I know this is the wrong response, but I can't stand the thought that Samantha might buy into her father's obviously gratuitous behavior—especially since it doesn't seem to bother him when the tuition hasn't been paid or his child-support check is late."

"Have you spoken with your ex-husband about this?" I asked.

"Oh sure," she said bitterly. "He accuses me of being jealous. He says why shouldn't he buy her things, since it gives them both so much pleasure. I tell him he could do more for her by making sure his payments are on time, but he doesn't get it."

Eve is in a tough situation. She can't persuade her ex-husband to be a responsible parent. And she can't prevent him from giving Samantha what she asks for. All Eve can do is let her daughter know that she can't buy the Barbie outfit. It doesn't help to criticize her ex, and doesn't help to blame her daughter for the fact that her father buys her things she can't afford. It is hard to find ways of communicating your values without putting down your ex. But Eve might say "Your father and I don't see eye to eye on this matter" and let it go at that.

Sometimes the tug-of-war is more subtle, as Judy described in this incident with her son, Andrew, twelve. Andrew had had a bad cold all week, and as Friday drew near, Judy told him that she wanted him to stay home that weekend and rest, instead of going to his father's house. He reacted with rage.

ANDREW: You can't make me stay home!

JUDY: Your health is more important than going to your father's. You've already missed several days of school this semester, and I don't want you to miss any more.

ANDREW: You bitch!

JUDY (furious): Don't you dare talk to me that way! As long as you live under my roof, you'll obey my rules.

ANDREW: I don't have to! I'm going to Dad's.

JUDY (out of control): Good! Then pack your things. Go live with your dad. I'm through taking this shit from you!

Judy storms out, goes into her room, and slams the door. She sits on the bed shaking, feeling overwhelmed with a mixture of fury and remorse. After about a half hour, Andrew comes into the room.

ANDREW: Let's not go to bed angry.
JUDY: I can't help but be upset at what happened. No matter how mad you are, you can't insult me like you did.
ANDREW: But *you* really upset *me* tonight. It really hurt me a lot when you said I should just pack my bags and leave. I was worried that you might kick me out. [Starts to cry.]
JUDY: I feel terrible that I said that—and I don't mean it. But I too was hurt. I guess when we're upset we really know how to wound each other. I shouldn't have said what I did. I guess I need to know that you appreciate me sometimes. I should have let you decide about going to your dad's this weekend. You're old enough to know if you feel well enough.
ANDREW (giving her a hug): Okay, Mom. I'll miss you when I'm gone.
JUDY (squeezing him tight): I'll miss you, too. I always miss you when you're not here.

This is a good example of how even when we use words to hurt and demean, we can, once removed and calm, open up lines of communication and express the loving feelings behind the outburst.

The Lonely Parent

When we imagine ourselves as parents, there is always another adult in the picture—the husband or wife who will make the unit complete. This "other" is our adult support system, a shoulder to cry on when things get tough, someone to share the burden and the joys, or just to take over when we're too stressed or exhausted. But often the single parents who attend my workshops are women who alone bear most of the responsibility for their children, and feel as though they are doing it all without support or appreciation. Linda, a recently divorced mother, who was feeling very lonely and vulnerable, told this story of how her daughter sabotaged an opportunity for her to get help from a friend.

"A few months ago, my daughter and I moved to a different apartment. It was not a move either of us wanted to make. We had lived in our former apartment for many years—since my daughter, Lynne, was born, and after the divorce we remained there. Now the landlord's daughter was getting married and wanted the apartment, so we had to leave. We moved in January—there was snow on the ground. Lynne, who is eight, was very saddened by the move. I knew this, so I let her have a friend over to play while I worked with the movers. I had been up since five that morning packing boxes. My friend Barry had offered to help take down my fixtures, and he said he would call in the early afternoon, but the call never came—or so I thought.

"When I finally called Barry in the evening to ask what had happened to him, he told me he had called while I had been downstairs with the movers, and had spoken to Lynne. 'She told me not to come over, that you didn't need the help after all,' he told me. I couldn't believe my daughter had actually said that, knowing how much I *did* need help. When I got off the phone, I confronted her. 'Lynne, how could you have lied to Barry like that?'

"Lynne denied that she had told Barry not to come over, but her friend, Alice, piped up, 'Yes, you did. You did too say that.'

"I was stressed out and enraged, and when Alice went home, I verbally attacked Lynne. 'You're so selfish, how could you be so selfish?' I repeated over and over. I felt so sorry for myself. Lynne doesn't understand how hard it is to be alone and have to take responsibility for everything all by myself. I suppose if I had been able to be more understanding, I would have realized that Lynne was threatened by Barry's presence, but to tell you the truth, sometimes it's so tough and I feel so overwhelmed that I'm not always in the mood to be too understanding. It's hard for me to be sensitive to her needs all the time when no one is there for me."

Because they feel isolated and lonely, and are often lacking any form of support system, single parents may unintentionally make heavy demands on their children to be their companions and friends. As one mother reflected, "The hardest thing is letting go, especially since I sometimes feel lonely. I want us to share more. But I believe that children retreat from 'needy' parents. If we are personally fulfilled, they pick up on that and are more willing to be open with us. Right now, I am going through a time of major change, both personally and professionally, and I sometimes feel very vulnerable and alone. I'm trying not to lean on my kids too much, but when there's no one else . . ."

It's easy to forget that our children may be feeling lonely too. After all, we reason, they have us to take care of them. Shouldn't they be more understanding of our plight? Children by definition are self-involved and can't really put themselves in our shoes. This does not mean they are incapable of empathy, love, or generous gestures—just that their egocentricity is a basic reality.

I have heard parenting described as a "thankless" task, and often it seems that way. Many a parent has complained that their children do not seem to understand or appreciate all the time and effort that goes into making their lives better. So much energy and emotion is invested in trying to fill our children's needs and make them happy that sometimes we grow furious when children seem lacking in gratitude. Although all parents struggle with this, single parents can be particularly resentful about their children's self-centeredness, since they perceive their own sacrifices to be so great.

Mona, a single working mother, had saved her money for more than a year to take her nine-year-old son, Michael, on a week-long vacation to Disneyland. It was her way of making up to him for all the time she was unable to spend with him because of her work schedule. As the date of the trip grew closer, she became more and more excited, imagining how thrilled Michael would be by the fantastic sights and sounds she still remembered from her youth. But once they arrived at Disneyland, things turned out quite differently from what she had expected. By the second day, Michael was dragging his feet and complaining that he was tired of doing so much walking. By the third day he was whining "I'm bored" and asking when they were going to go home. The final blow came when he said, "Why did we have to come here? I would rather have spent my vacation playing with my friends."

Mona was crushed by Michael's reaction to the vacation she had worked so hard to provide. His absence of delight and gratitude made her furious. How could he behave this way after all she had done for him?

As parents, we feel that we have earned our children's love and gratitude—especially when, like Mona, we go out of our way to give them something special. Single parents may need the affirmation even more, as "proof" that a child doesn't resent them for the family's breakup. But sometimes it happens that what we give children reflects our idea of fun, not theirs, or is what we want for them, not what they want for themselves.

Mothers in this situation talk about what a relief it is to complain or share their problems with others who are in the same boat. No one should have to bear the burden of parenthood without others to support and empathize with them—a shoulder to cry on, a person to lean on.

Making Peace as a Family

We think of divorce as a permanent separation, the end of a relationship. But when children are in the picture, the couple is never completely separated. It is this fact that many divorcing parents find so hard to accept. "I resent that I have to deal with my ex-husband civilly," one mother admitted. "And it really upsets me when I see how much my children idolize their father. When they return from visits, I have to grit my teeth to keep from telling them, 'You think he's so great. If only you knew!' "

Anita and her husband, George, had joint custody of their six-year-old son, Barney. That meant that Barney stayed with his father two or three days a week and with his mother on the alternate days. Nevertheless, Anita often complained that she felt overwhelmed by the responsibilities of single parenthood.

"I'm wondering why you are feeling so burdened," I said. "I thought you had joint custody."

"We do—if you can call it that," she said and laughed. "My ex-husband is very irresponsible. I still have to remind him about everything. When Barney is with him, I usually call several times to remind him to give Barney his medicine or not let him go out without a coat. I can't trust him to do things right."

It seemed that Anita was having a hard time letting go of a role she had played with her husband when they were married. I mentioned this to her. "What do you think will happen if you don't remind your ex-husband to do those things while Barney is in his care—and just let him be in charge for the days they are together?"

Her eyes grew large. "Are you kidding? I don't want to imagine what will happen."

"But doesn't joint custody imply that there is a sharing of responsibility?"

"Yes, but you don't know my ex."

I wondered out loud what would be the worst thing that could happen if Anita's forgetful ex didn't do everything according to her standards. She shuddered and said she wasn't willing to find out.

Anita is perhaps unaware of the extent to which she has assigned the role "incompetent parent" to her ex. Perhaps he is less efficient than she, but I could not help being reminded of many instances in which mothers complained about their husbands' being unhelpful; however, as soon as the men did take charge, these women criticized them for "doing it all wrong."

We can't address all the many complex issues raised by families who struggle with divorce. I have tremendous admiration for the single parents who are giving 150 percent to the task of raising their children—and who are battling valiantly to be good parents in spite of daily assaults to their self-esteem. Instead of admiring the single parent (usually mother) for her dedication, society focuses on the shattered ideal and reinforces her sense of aloneness. It is natural that these parents—overwhelmed, exhausted, embittered, and lonely—should feel a great deal of anger over the fundamental unfairness of their plight. And it is just as natural that their children sometimes feel angry and sad too. Shirley, a mother in my single-parent workshop, recalled a Sunday afternoon after her five-year-old daughter returned from a weekend with her father. "Gloom hung over the house like a cloud," she said. "I walked into the living room, and Jill was slumped on the couch looking like she had just lost her best friend. My heart went out to her. I realized how lately I had been so wrapped up in my own problems, I had not been thinking very much about the way she was feeling. I went over and sat down beside her and put my arms around her. My anger toward her father, who had been making my life miserable, lessened as I realized how much she loved him. I didn't have to love him to acknowledge that. I said, 'You're sad because Daddy's gone, aren't you?' She nodded. I said, 'Daddy loves you very much, and he's sad when he's not with you, too. But before you know it, next weekend will be here and you can be together again.' Jill looked at me with such gratitude as I said those words. I was aware that they were the first kind words I had said about her father since the divorce, and she needed so much to hear them. By momentarily putting aside my own hard feelings, I had made life possible again for my daughter."

6

High Hopes and Shattered Expectations

Einstein's parents feared their son was retarded because he spoke haltingly until the age of nine and thereafter would respond to questions only after a long period of deliberation. He performed so badly in all high school courses except mathematics that a teacher asked him to drop out, telling him, "You will never amount to anything, Einstein."

—from "Celebrated Persons Who Had
Miserable Report Cards,"
People's Almanac

Alberta, a parent in my workshop, once related with great honesty and self-awareness a conversation that had taken place with her eight-year-old son, Troy. She had found him playing with his transformers one afternoon when he was supposed to be practicing the piano. He was performing in a class recital later that week. "Troy," she said, "if you don't practice, you won't get a gold star." He looked moodily up from his toys. "*You* want me to get a star, right?" he challenged her. Without hesitation, she nodded, "Yes, I do." He laughed. "Okay, Mom, I'll practice."

Most parents want their children to be achievers—this

is only natural. And yet, I have found that one of the primary sources of conflict in families has to do with this desire, especially when the expectations are unrealistic, or when we have trouble separating our needs from our children's. How many of us were brought up on the refrain, "It's for your own good"—a refrain we automatically repeat with our own children? Alberta's exchange with Troy was interesting because in that moment, she recognized how pleased *she* would be to sit in the audience and watch Troy perform beautifully. It's a perfectly natural response. "I knew he would also be disappointed if he didn't get a star," she added. "But in that moment, it was about me wanting him to get a star, and I admitted it." She laughed. "I think he was so surprised by my admission that he became agreeable."

"Why do you think that is?" I asked.

She thought for a minute. "I don't know. Maybe because he expected the usual lecture about how I knew how much *he* wanted to win an award."

I nodded. "Yes. And just then, he didn't experience wanting it. What he wanted was to play. Often, parents make proclamations that are based on what they want for their children, but the children don't always agree—or even understand. I once heard a mother tell her eight-year-old son, 'If you don't start paying attention to your schoolwork, you'll never get into college.' He looked at her as though she were speaking a foreign language."

It is hard for parents to admit that sometimes the frustration they experience with their children stems from their own fantasies and hopes. They slide easily from "we" to "you" in conversations because, quite naturally, they want their offspring to be all that they can be (and perhaps all that they themselves have not been able to be). It's natural to have expectations for one's children, but when they are too high or articulated too rigidly, it creates friction. Children either resent what they perceive to be unreasonable demands, or they suffer trying to please their parents, at the expense of their own sense of identity.

One of the problems with expecting great things is the disappointment that comes when these expectations are not met. Sometimes we express anger toward our children when they are difficult, having problems, or not conforming to the expected norm. Rita, the parent of a five-year-old boy, expressed her frustration that Sam seemed more dependent upon her and less willing to separate from her than the other children in his kindergarten class. She was feeling very anxious the day she brought it up in the group, because the following week she was taking Sam to an interview at a private elementary school and she wanted him to present himself well. She admitted that the pressure she felt was making her angry with her son.

Sam was a creative, sensitive, loving, easily frightened little boy. He was enormously imaginative and playful, but a little bit behind his peers in being able to let go of his mother. She was worried that Sam wouldn't be accepted by the school, and she felt guilty about the way her anxiety manifested itself in anger toward her son.

I told her about having experienced a similar problem with my son Todd. "Todd was a child who marched to his own drummer," I said. "But I was so focused on his fitting in that I often got frustrated when he did things differently. I remember when he was eight, he only wanted to play with kids who were a few years younger. It worried me. Why couldn't Todd play with kids his own age, like 'normal' boys did? But at the time, that was what made him feel good. The younger boys looked up to him, and he needed that. He wasn't doing anything harmful. But in my anxiety about his being 'different,' I concluded that an eight-year-old should play with eight-year-olds. I was sorely tempted to criticize him by saying 'What's wrong with you? Why can't you play with kids your own age? Why do you always have to play with little kids when there are so many boys your own age around?' Fortunately, someone wiser pointed out to me that what he was doing was not only perfectly harmless, but it probably enhanced his self-confidence. This realization helped me to back off and leave him be."

Rita's anger is tied into her disappointment about Sam's being different from the kids in his class. She's understandably afraid he won't be accepted—worried that he'll screw up in the interview. And beneath her fear, she is probably thinking "Why can't he be an easier, more normal child—more like the other kids, who seem so comfortable in new situations—why does he have to be fearful and clingy?" But while Rita is concerned about Sam's future and how he will do in the stressful years ahead, what she is inadvertently communicating to her son is that there's something wrong with him.

It's so easy for us to get stuck in false ideals for our children, ideals based on what we've heard from others or the way we've seen others behave. We're embarrassed if our children don't seem to be doing as well as we imagine other children are doing. We think if our kids get into a certain school, which everyone says is a "top" school, the school will ensure our child's success. But maybe Sam isn't ready yet, and a different, less pressured environment would be more suitable.

Rita needed to stop focusing on the ways that Sam was *different* (and therefore less capable) from the other children, and start focusing on the ways that he was *special.* He might have been developmentally behind many of the other boys in his class, but Sam did possess a number of very appealing qualities. Rita was unable to appreciate those positive qualities because she was too busy noticing Sam's differentness.

Often children need special help when they don't easily adjust to their environment. But what constitutes real help? Sometimes when we think we are helping them, we are inadvertently communicating to them that they have let us down by not accomplishing what we think they should. This message can damage a child's self-esteem. Dorothy Corkille Briggs, a noted expert on the subject of self-esteem in children, writes in *Experts Advise Parents*, "If a child believes he is unlovable or lovable only on condition, he may develop all kinds of competence. However, these skills are hollow victories. No amount of competence ever substitutes for lovability. . . . Each child needs to be cherished for his sheer existence." So the question becomes: How can we learn to set aside our disappointment and relate to our children as unique individuals with special needs of their own?

Almost all of the parents who take my workshops are highly motivated to see their children do well. Often, they heap the kids' plates high with cultural and educational experiences. They'll speak proudly of the ways their children excel in many activities, and sometimes it concerns them when their children would rather play Nintendo than visit museums or take ballet or music lessons. I tell them that their reactions are perfectly understandable, but remind them that when they want something for their children more than the children want it for themselves, it can backfire.

Janice was challenged on this point by her son, Gary. Gary, seven, had to work on "achievements" for Cub Scouts, which were due on Thursday. In order to get the award he so longed for at an upcoming Scout dinner, he had to complete certain tasks by that day. But Gary was a procrastinator—what seven-year-old is not? Now it was the weekend before the dinner, and Gary's mother, Janice, was starting to get nervous that he might not complete the achievements in time. She related this incident in one of my workshops.

JANICE: Gary, you have to work on your Cub Scout achievements this weekend. Would you like to do them on Saturday or on Sunday?

GARY: I'll do them on Sunday.

JANICE: Okay, but don't forget.

[Sunday morning arrives.]

JANICE: Gary, it's time to do your Cub Scout work.

GARY: I don't want to. It's boring.

JANICE (getting angry and raising her voice): Gary, we had a deal. You said you'd do your achievements today. Now get moving!

GARY (really whining): I won't have time for any fun or play. It will take *all* day. It's not fair!

JANICE: If you'd just get busy now, it shouldn't take more than an hour. You'll have the rest of the day to play.

GARY: That's too long! I don't want to.

JANICE (frustrated and mad): Maybe you don't *want* to be a Cub Scout.

GARY: No, I do.

JANICE: Then, be responsible. Do your work!

GARY (starting to cry): I don't *want* to. I want to play.

JANICE (starting to yell): Gary, you have three choices: One, do your work and get a bead [the reward] at the Scout dinner. Two, don't do it, and you won't get an award. Three, quit Cub Scouts, and then you won't have to be *bothered* with any of it.

GARY: No! Those aren't good choices. I want to play!

JANICE: You've put this off for weeks, and we had a deal. Just do it.

GARY: Why are you so mean! You're always telling me what to do. Why do I have to?

JANICE: Because I know, come Thursday, you'll be upset when you don't get a bead and your friends do.

GARY (yelling): No! *You* will. You'll be upset.

JANICE (totally taken aback): Do you really think I will be upset?

GARY: Yes!

JANICE (calmer now): Gary, would you like to quit the Scouts?

GARY (also calmer): No . . . not really.

JANICE: Okay, Gary. What you are saying is *very* interesting. Why don't you think about your choices and what *you* really want to do. I'll leave you alone to make your own decision.

Janice left the room to do other things. After a few minutes, Gary started to work on his achievements. On Thursday night at the award dinner, Gary earned two beads. Only five boys out of twenty-six received two beads.

JANICE: You must be very proud of yourself.

GARY: Yes . . . are you proud of me too?

JANICE (hugging him): I'm always proud of you, whether you get beads or not. But this calls for a very special celebration. Let's go get ice-cream sundaes.

GARY: Great! I love you, Mom.

The group and I were full of admiration for Janice's ability to step back and distance herself enough from her son to really help him. And Gary helped her do this by reminding her that it was *his* job to decide about doing the Cub Scout work and getting the beads. It isn't easy to stand aside and let our children grapple with their own responsibilities, but when our pressuring becomes interference, we rob them of their independence and the sense of achievement that comes from doing well on their own.

Wanting the Best

One day I told my workshop group, "One of the hardest things I struggle with to this day—and I imagine you, too, will be struggling with for the rest of your lives—is the question of how often our well-meaning suggestions are experienced by our children as criticism or pressure to be different." Expectations are normal, as are our fantasies. But there is a need for us to re-examine our expectations constantly, asking ourselves where we end and our children begin. Kids, in order to separate, can't just be a "chip off the old block"—a reflection of us.

Fred, a father in the group, smiled. "That reminds me of a true story about a couple I know who have just had a baby, and they're already going around checking out the best schools to find out how their child can get in. So they went to the headmaster of a highly regarded school and asked, 'What should we do to make sure our child will have a good chance of getting into this school?' And the head-master said, 'Don't drop him.' "

Everyone laughed, but Lela, the mother of two young girls, said with a concerned look on her face, "But isn't our job as parents to try to groom our children for success and teach them how to compete? It's the kind of world we live in."

"I think we have to talk about it on a per-case basis," I said. "We need to be able to distinguish between riding roughshod over our children's feelings, and teaching them coping mechanisms and skills that help them to feel more competent."

"Well, what do you think about this," Lela continued. "I signed up my three-year-old daughter, Hope, for gymnastics because I thought it would be good for her. The teacher is quite strict and expects the children to wait their turns patiently. At first, Hope hated it. It was torture to take her to class. But now she seems to be fitting in better. It's good discipline, because she has to learn to sit quietly and wait her turn."

I said doubtfully, "The only way an active, bouncy three-year-old is going to stand for that is if she loves the activity so much she's willing to give up acting like a three-year-old."

"Well, most of the other three-year-olds do it," Lela said defensively. "They're much more docile and well-behaved. They don't seem to have the same trouble following instructions that Hope does."

"I'm a bit concerned when I hear about a three-year-old being docile, especially with your description of a strict teacher," I replied gently. "Perhaps the other children are conforming better than Hope because they're more fearful of the repercussions. Learning obedience is necessary, but is it appropriate in the situation you have described? We have to be very careful about the message we're sending. We have to listen to whether or not our children are agreeable to what we ask them to do, or if they're just responding out of fear, or even the need not to disappoint or anger us."

"But there's still the issue of wanting our children to learn certain values," said Fred, whose son is eight. "I've always had the philosophy that if you start something, you should stick with it. My son wanted to take karate, so we signed him up, and then he didn't like his teacher and wanted to quit. But I forced him to continue, because you can't just start something and then decide you don't like it, or change your mind in midstream."

"I wonder," I said, musing, "if this idea that always having to finish what you start is what stops a person from being a quitter." Certainly, that was my parents' conviction when I was growing up. Of course, we don't want our children to flit arbitrarily from one learning experience to another, without giving it their best shot. But can we allow them the privilege of sometimes changing their minds? Fred may also be thinking that karate is a good sport for little boys because boys should learn how to be tough. He had complained a few weeks earlier about how his son acted kind of wimpy.

"I guess I have to admit that I do want him to be 'all boy,' " said Fred. "It was the way I was raised. Maybe I'm being a little hard on him."

Fred's reaction is entirely normal. But if his son is totally unmotivated to excel in sports, he needs to respect that and take his son's wishes seriously. Exposing children to new experiences is not the same as forcing them to perform when they're really turned off.

Many children are quick to learn how to please their parents—which is not entirely bad. But in some households, the message gets communicated that failure to meet parental expectations will result in deep disappointment and sometimes punishment. When this happens, children sometimes harbor a deep resentment. I remember hearing the story of a young man who graduated from medical school. His father, who was himself a prominent surgeon, sat in the audience at the graduation ceremony bursting with pride. But when his son received the diploma, he marched up to his father and shoved it into his hands. "Here," he said. "You wanted it so badly—you keep it!" The young man did not go on to become a doctor. Imagine the rage he must have felt to go through medical school in order to defy his father by saying, "I'm never going to be the way you want me to be."

Often, it's not that parents are cruel or deliberately pushy. But sometimes a negative message gets through, as Lauren discovered with her thirteen-year-old son, Charles. Lauren brought her problem to my workshop group one morning.

"Charles has never excelled as a student, and his father and I have tried everything we could think of to help him. The fact is, he's lazy. He doesn't push himself when it comes to schoolwork, and he leaves things until the last minute. I try not to nag, but sometimes I can't help myself. Last month, the deadline was approaching for a report I knew was due on the Civil War, and I hadn't seen him working on it. Finally, I couldn't keep my mouth shut another minute. I was angry with him for always putting me in the position of having to nag him, and I couldn't help comparing him unfavorably to his younger brother, Darius, who is an excellent student. I said pretty sharply, 'Charles, you haven't started your report. How do you expect to get a good grade if you leave it until the last minute?' He immediately grew defensive and answered back, 'How do you know I haven't started it? I have too. I'm almost done with it. Leave me alone.'

"I backed off, but I didn't believe him. The next afternoon he came in and said, 'I'm working on my report, and I'm going to go over to Randolph's house. He did a report on the Civil War last year, and he's going to give me some advice.' I didn't think anything of it. I was just glad to see him getting serious about his work. A couple of days later, the day before the report was due, Charles told me he had done it, and asked me if I wanted to read it. I started reading, and my heart just sank. It was a spectacular report—there's just no way that Charles could have written it by himself. I realized then that he had copied Randolph's work. I wanted to attack him on the spot. I was furious that he would do something so wrong. At the same time, I know how lacking he is in confidence—he's always accusing me of favoring his brother or telling me that nothing he does is ever good enough—and I wasn't sure how to handle this. So I held off discussing it, at least temporarily. Yesterday, he came home and showed me his grade. The teacher had written 'A-plus-plus' in big red letters on the top. Now I don't know what to do. Charles could use a break—a little praise for a change. But how can I praise him when I know he did not write the report? I'm disappointed and angry with him, and I'm not sure how to handle the situation. What do you think I should do?"

The group exchanged ideas about Lauren's dilemma. "He must have felt pretty desperate to do that," I observed.

"He knows how important grades are to us," Lauren said. "His younger brother has never been a problem. He always gets good grades, and things just seem to come easily to him. But Charles has always been a difficult child, and I guess it's true that we're disappointed that he can't be more like his brother. Maybe we push him too hard. But to cheat is such an awful solution on his part."

"I can understand how you feel," said Mary, who has a thirteen-year-old daughter. "Julie has been having trouble in history this term, and I saw firsthand how scared it made her when she thought about how furious we'd be over a bad report card. She was very upset the day she received it, and she warned me we were going to be very angry at her when we read the report card. I wrote down what happened."

I urged Mary to read the dialogue she had prepared, hoping it would shed some light on Lauren's dilemma.

MOM: You seem to be very upset and disappointed in your report card.
JULIE: You and Daddy are going to be so mad!
MOM: Let's look at it, then we'll talk about what to do.
JULIE (handing her the report card): Well, here it is.
[The card revealed that Julie had failed history and gotten a C − in her science finals.]
MOM: You did very well in English, math, art, and physical education. I know you're upset about history and science. We need to discuss how you can improve in these subjects.

But when Marvin saw the report card, he was furious that she had failed history and done so poorly in science.

MARVIN: Either she is not putting in the time and effort, or the school isn't doing a good job teaching. I'm not paying over seven thousand dollars for private school if this is the best I can expect. Maybe she'd be better off in a public school.
MARY: I know you're feeling angry, but let's not make any rash decisions until we've had some time to think further about this.

"The next evening, calmer and feeling more objective, we had a family meeting to discuss what Julie could do to improve her history and science grades. But what really struck me about the incident was how fearful Julie was of our disapproval. She felt guilty about how much money we were spending on the school, and she was concerned that she wasn't measuring up and that we might make her change schools."

Lauren was thoughtful. "You have a point, Mary. I can see how worried Charles is about our disappointment—especially since his brother gets so much praise from us. I need to handle this matter of his cheating sensitively. But I also have to be firm."

I suggested to Lauren that she talk to Charles or even write him a note. "Communicate that you feel this is very serious and that you've thought a lot about it. Say something like 'I know how important this report was or you wouldn't have taken such drastic measures.' Then explain what plagiarism is and why it's an unacceptable solution, no matter how desperate he felt."

Lauren agreed to do this, and the next week she returned to the group and related this exchange between herself and Charles:

LAUREN: I'm concerned because I don't think you wrote the report about the Civil War by yourself.

CHARLES: What do you mean? I did too.

LAUREN: It didn't sound like you. Did you use some of your friend's words?

[Charles looks down at the table and doesn't answer.]

LAUREN: I realize you must have felt pretty desperate to take such extreme measures. Why don't we talk about that.

CHARLES: I didn't copy the whole report, just a little. I couldn't do it alone. I really tried, but it was so complicated.

LAUREN: Why didn't you tell me you were having trouble?

CHARLES: You probably would have been mad and told me I should study more.

LAUREN: Charles, your father and I want you to do your

best in school, but we don't expect you to do more than you can. Copying another person's work is not the answer. What do you think we should do?

CHARLES (alarmed): Are you going to tell the teacher?

LAUREN: I'm not sure, but the point is that you and I have to decide how we're going to prevent this from happening again.

"We then went on to have a conversation about studying, and we came up with a plan that for now Charles would show me his homework every day. If he had problems understanding the material, he agreed to go to his teacher and talk about getting special help."

Lauren sighed. "It was so hard to figure out how to express my concerns without really hurting Charles. I was even tempted not to say anything at all, and to give him his small moment in the sun. But I feel good about the agreement we reached. In the long run, it's much better for Charles to know that what he did was wrong and to see that there are other options. I also learned just how important it is for him to feel that he's doing well in our eyes. I'm going to concentrate on finding ways to praise him for the things he does do well."

All parents want their children to excel in school, and when they have problems, it is hard to be objective. Parent-teacher conferences are often the source of disappointment, embarrassment, or even rage when a child's performance doesn't measure up. What parent does not dream about a child's teacher heaping glowing praise, only to find complaints instead? Teachers are the experts, aren't they? They should know what they're talking about. When they praise our children, it makes us proud. But often parent-teacher conferences create intense anxiety and frustration for parents. As one mother told me, "I walked into the meeting loving my child, and walked out hating him." Parents have often said that when they visit their children's classrooms, they feel themselves transported back to the days when they were students. They want approval from the teachers. But they also want to be their child's ally, and often are put in the uncomfortable position of being caught in the middle between teacher and child.

Susan told the group about her son's teacher, who told her Aaron was immature and insecure. "I was immediately defensive. I asked her, 'On what do you base those labels?' She said she was showing a movie about Africa in which there were bare-breasted women, and Aaron got hysterical, falling out of his chair with laughter. That was an example of his immaturity. I thought it sounded like pretty normal ten-year-old behavior, but the teacher told me that he should have demonstrated better self-control. Maybe it wasn't normal, and I was just being defensive. I felt embarrassed, and I later told Aaron that it was inappropriate behavior for him to disrupt the class. But the incident left me feeling frustrated and angry at both my son and his teacher. On the one hand, I hated to be in the position of having the teacher express her disappointment about my child. But on the other hand, I felt I should have defended him more."

"If the teacher calls, my husband and I immediately think 'What's wrong?' " said Katherine, the mother of three. "All we have to hear is that the teacher is calling on the phone, and we get upset. It's like 'Your teacher is calling. What did you do wrong?' Wouldn't it be wonderful if teachers would sometimes call to tell us how much they enjoy our children or to report something positive? Both teachers and parents seem to be so focused on what the child is doing wrong—instead of on the things they are doing right."

It's helpful for both parents and teachers to step back

and recognize that they are allies, not adversaries, in the education of children. They share the same goals. It is not a power struggle. The issue is not who has the most authority; it's how best to resolve the behavior and learning problems that children have. These problems are more easily resolved when parents and teachers work together.

Lies and Betrayal

It is sometimes even harder to accept our children when they let us down not by accident but deliberately. We don't know how to react, except with anger, when they betray our trust or lie to us about important things.

Heather related the story of the day she learned that her thirteen-year-old daughter, Roberta, had been playing hooky from school. The discovery came by accident. Roberta's math teacher called her one morning at work and expressed his concern that Roberta was missing so much material during a crucial segment. "I don't understand," Heather replied, puzzled.

"Well, Roberta has already missed three days this month, and I decided to call you, since she was out again today," the math teacher said.

Heather remembers her reaction. "A dead weight descended into my stomach. I said, as calmly as I could, 'As far as I know, Roberta is in school today. If she's not, that means she's playing hooky.' "

"I went over the attendance record with the teacher and wrote down the dates Roberta had been absent. Only one of them was legitimate. I had no idea where she had been the other days.

"I left the office early, because I wanted to be home when Roberta got there. I was furious with her, but also scared. Was she having a problem I hadn't recognized? I felt guilty that something so big could have been going on right under my nose, and I hadn't seen it. And then I started feeling embarrassed. How could she humiliate me this way in front of her teachers? They would all think I was a lousy mother because I hadn't even noticed that something was wrong."

Heather recalled the conversation that occurred as soon as her daughter walked in the door.

ROBERTA (surprised to see her mother): Mom! Did you get off work early today?

HEATHER (still calm): Yes. How was school today?

ROBERTA (cheerfully): Oh, fine.

HEATHER: Roberta, sit down.

ROBERTA: Is something wrong?

HEATHER: I know you didn't go to school today.

ROBERTA (face falling): I can explain.

HEATHER (sarcastically): And can you also explain the other days this month that you weren't at school?

ROBERTA (miserably): Oh . . . I knew you'd find out. I feel awful.

HEATHER (screaming now): You feel awful? That's all you have to say for yourself? I was so humiliated when Mr. Madison called. My daughter playing hooky! I couldn't believe it. I want an explanation for this, young lady.

ROBERTA (starting to cry): I'm sorry, Mom. I was bored and the weather was nice, and Janice and I went down to the mall. I knew it was wrong. I promise you, I'll never do it again.

HEATHER: How can I believe that? How will I ever be able to trust you again? You have ruined everything. I thought you were a good kid, but now I see I was wrong. Just go to your room. I don't even want to look at you—and you're grounded for a month.

In these circumstances, Heather was unable to put aside her feelings of having been betrayed in order to address objectively what Roberta had done. Her personal disappointment overshadowed everything, so the message that was communicated to Roberta was that she was bad because she had let her down and embarrassed her. There was no room in this dialogue to talk about Roberta's actions and why they were unacceptable. Nor was there an effort to figure out why she was playing hooky and to go about finding ways to solve the problem. It wasn't that Heather didn't want to do these things. She simply did not know how to express the extreme seriousness of Roberta's behavior in a way that was not accusatory and punitive.

Consider, for example, what Heather was feeling when she learned of Roberta's truancy. As she described it, there were a number of emotions. First, she was frightened—she didn't know where her daughter was. Second, she was worried that Roberta had a big problem, and her worry was accompanied by guilt because she thought she should have seen it. Third, she was embarrassed—surely the teachers would think she was a terrible parent for allowing this to happen. Finally, she felt helpless, a feeling that often leads to rage. She had believed she was in control, and she was not.

When she confronted Roberta, all of these emotions were raging inside her. She could hardly be blamed for feeling that way, but her rage prevented her from addressing the crisis rationally. As a result, nothing was settled. It would have been more helpful if she had waited until she calmed down to confront Roberta, rather than accost her as soon as she walked in the door. She might have had more success learning what precipitated the hooky playing, and they might have been more ready to discuss appropriate actions to take and meaningful consequences.

When children let us down, deceive us, or flout our wishes, it is very hard not to let our imaginations (and our mouths!) run away with us. We tend to universalize their actions and make dire predictions for the future:

You're *always* getting into trouble.
You *never* do what I say.
I'll never be able to trust you again.
Keep this up, and you'll be a failure.

Parents also have a habit of futurizing actions that occur in the present. For example, Deidre, the mother of a teen-age boy, drew inappropriate conclusions when she found her son not doing his homework as he had promised. Not only did she make broad assumptions about his behavior in general, she made assumptions about the kind of person he would become in the future. Here is Deidre's description of the incident.

"My son, who is fourteen, has a job on Monday evenings delivering for a fast-food place in the neighborhood. I let him do it, but we made a rule that on Mondays he has to come right home from school and do his homework because he wouldn't be free to do it in the evening. So, last Monday, he came home from school, and I heard music coming from his room. So I knocked on his door and said, 'You're listening to music. You're not doing your homework.' I started out okay. I reminded him calmly about our agreement and asked him why he was listening to music instead of doing what he was supposed to be doing. And he just sort of shrugged and said something about not having much homework. Then I got mad because I didn't believe him, and I started in on him: 'This just figures! I should have known that you wouldn't keep our agreement. If your grades are bad, you'll have to quit your job.' Now, I had no real reason to believe that his grades would be bad. But by the end of my screaming fit, I had practically accused him of flunking all his courses. And I said, 'At the rate you're going, all you'll be fit for is delivering Chinese food for a living.' Then he got mad, and he said, 'All you ever do is yell.' And I yelled, 'That's not true!' And we were both mad for the rest of the day. What struck me later, when I had calmed down, were all the assumptions I had made on the basis of such a small incident. I convinced myself that he was doing poorly in his courses just because for half an hour he was listening to music."

"Can you think of anything in particular that might have set you off?" I asked Deidre.

"I guess I worry a lot," she admitted. "And that day I had been reading an article in the newspaper about how colleges were becoming increasingly competitive. It intensified my fear that my son wouldn't be able to make it."

It's a script that seems to run through every parent's head automatically. When my older son, who is an adult, leaves for work late or oversleeps, I immediately jump to conclusions. It's such unhelpful thinking. If we parents could learn to stay in the moment, we'd be better off.

Deidre agreed that her behavior was totally unfair. "One minute we were talking about a specific situation, and the next minute I was making all these accusations related to the next twenty years of his life," she said. "He, of course, reacted with total disgust."

Deidre's expectations are the source of her frustration with her son. Even before our children are born, we have an expectation of what they will be like, and chances are that reality won't always match what we imagined. We may want our child to be a high achiever, and find that he's a dreamer. Or we may want an active sports-oriented child, and imagine about how great it will be to watch her play on the tennis team (perhaps because we never had the chance). Then we're disappointed when she'd rather be by herself reading a book or examining insects under a microscope. Sometimes we parents waste a lot of energy trying to fit square pegs into round holes. We have to be sensitive to the message we're sending. Very often, it's "I can't accept you the way you are. I can only accept you the way I want you to be." Although very normal, these "Be the way I want you to be" messages are hard on our children. We have to guard against what comes out sounding like constant criticism—"Sure, you can be elected class president, but when do you ever help around the house?"

A piece in *Mad* magazine made the point in a way that was humorous, yet really hit home. I read it to the group, and they laughed with recognition. A series of parent/child conversations were described this way:

What you say to your parents:	*What you hope they will say:*	*What they will proba say:*
Great news, Mom! I just got a full scholarship to Harvard!	Just think! An Ivy Leaguer in the family! I'm so happy I could cry!	Sure . . . you can g into an Ivy League school, but you car even keep your roo clean!
I've decided to join the Peace Corps.	That's really touching . . . my little girl devoting her life to helping those less fortunate than herself!	What are you goin; teach the Zambian: How to stay on the phone for hours an run up big bills?
I'm going to be a poetess . . . like Edna St. Vincent Millay!	And you will! You're so sensitive . . . so aware of the true meaning of life!	You'll make some poetess with your f breaking out from the junk you eat!

Unconditional love is extraordinarily difficult to achieve, since it can mean letting go of our fondest desires and dreams for our children. This is an age-old struggle; even Confucius asked, "Can there be a love which does not make demands on its object?" But for us as parents, it is a worthwhile goal to be open to our children's uniqueness, to support them even when they feel like failures, and to reinforce our love for who they are rather than what they do.

The "Special" Child Challenge

Eben was a premature baby and from the beginning, he faced a variety of physical problems. A staph infection shortly after birth turned into a life-threatening condition that involved occlusion of the main vein to the liver. For many years, Eben's life was a series of hospital stays, operations, and impediments to normal life. The operations were terrifying, and his mother, Sheila, a warm and compassionate woman, struggled to be strong for her son during the worst times.

"I was very intent on not 'knuckling under' from the pressure. I tried to keep a stiff upper lip. Once a nurse clinician commented on how perfect I was under pressure, and I preened. I didn't realize that in trying to be a model for Eben of courage and tenacity, I was also cutting him off from himself and from me. I never let him see my feelings of fatigue, rage, and despair. I would do my crying in the ladies' room down the hall. I was afraid of the feelings we had of 'What's going to happen to us?' Eben began to resent my inauthenticity, and I resented his resentment. After all, look at all I was doing for him! But he would say, 'I hate you,' as I left his room, or as they wheeled him off to the operating room."

For those of us who have been blessed with healthy

children, the pain and struggle of coping with a physically or mentally impaired child is impossible to imagine. The ordinary confrontations take on a life-and-death severity. For example, Sheila's fear that Eben would throw a tantrum, play too vigorously, or get involved in a fight in the school-yard was a valid one—these actions could be dangerous for him. On top of that, there are the feelings that never go away: guilt that the child's suffering might somehow be your fault, despair that this has happened to you (especially if it seems that it might have been avoided), exhaustion leading to anger over the never-ending crises, and resentment when your child does not appreciate your patience, love, and hard work.

Eben was naturally going to feel disappointed when he couldn't participate in the activities other children could. Sheila couldn't prevent that disappointment, but she could ease his frustration by acknowledging that she understood, saying, for example, "You want to climb on the jungle gym, and you're disappointed that you can't. I understand." Then she might distract him with another activity. This empathy could also help ease her own resentment that Eben wanted to do things he couldn't do, and help her give him permission to want things, even though he couldn't have them.

No parent is prepared to face these special circumstances. Most of us, who have never had to, can't imagine how we would manage. In *After the Tears: Parents Talk About Raising a Child with a Disability*, by Robin Simons, many parents admit that the deeply felt emotions of rage, unfairness, and resentment never completely go away. Even the strongest parents could find their anger triggered anew by a reminder that their disabled child would never experience—or share with them—the normal daily pleasures. But, notes Simons, even though the feelings don't go away, they do diminish somewhat. "For some," she writes, "that process begins with

letting go of the 'why'—releasing the need to find an answer
for why it happened to you and accepting the fact that it
did." As one parent in the book related, "At the beginning
I was so angry—at fate, at God, at life, even at Mark [the
disabled child]—because this had happened to us. It seemed
so senseless. The handicap seemed so overwhelming—that
was all I saw. But now, compared to who Mark is as a
person, the handicap is secondary. I still get sad and angry
about it; I wish he didn't have it. But everything about his
handicap is so much easier to handle now because it's all
a part of *him*."

Children do not need to have severe handicaps for parents to feel frustrated and confused. We now know that
learning disabilities are quite common, though not always
easy to identify or deal with. Charlotte and Bruce, a couple
who came to one of my workshops, expressed their feelings
of helplessness when they learned their seven-year-old son,
Patrick, had a learning disability. Like all parents, Charlotte
and Bruce had high hopes for their child, and now they
saw these hopes being shattered as they watched Patrick
struggle with even the most elementary learning.

"When we first found out that Patrick had a problem,
we said 'Okay, we'll deal with it,' said Charlotte. "Bruce
and I are doers—we're not the kind of people to be stopped
by challenges. We decided we'd work with Patrick, give
him lots of extra attention, and together overcome his
handicap. We read everything we could get our hands on,
and talked to specialists."

"I think we were naive," added Bruce. "We thought we
could 'cure' Patrick. We didn't really grasp that his disability
would be an ongoing struggle."

"What was your reaction when it finally dawned on you?"
I asked.

"It was a horrible realization," said Charlotte quietly.

"Patrick is such a sweet boy, but even so we found ourselves growing impatient."

"And resentful," said Bruce. "I don't like myself very much for the things I thought. Secretly, I blamed Patrick for the problems he was having at school. His teacher wasn't very knowledgeable about his disability, and often, when he gave an offbeat answer, she thought he was being a wise guy. Or she'd suggest he wasn't trying hard enough. I kept thinking 'Maybe she's right. He's not trying.' Then I'd be impatient."

"Bruce and I fought about it a lot," said Charlotte. "Poor Patrick! Both at school and at home, he was hearing that there was something wrong with him."

"How did you resolve the problem?" I asked.

"We finally decided to get counseling," said Charlotte. "We were recommended to a specialist who works with learning-disabled children. When we met with her, she let us get out all of our frustration and rage, and she told us that it was okay to feel the way we did. That was a tremendous relief. She also let us know that Patrick's disability was not our fault, nor was it something we could 'cure.' We had been blaming ourselves, and also blaming him, but we learned to view this as a blameless situation."

"We wish Patrick didn't have a learning disability, but we're growing more accepting of it," said Bruce. "He deserves our full support and compassion, and we're helping him feel worthwhile and proud of himself, even though he's different from his peers."

Giving Affirmation

Dean, the father of a twelve-year-old boy, said, "My son is so sloppy, it drives me crazy. I try hard not to criticize, and when I can't restrain myself, it backfires. In fact, he reacts by getting sarcastic with me. He says, 'Thanks a lot, Dad. I guess you expect me to be perfect.' It takes me back to when I was a kid. Nothing I ever did was good enough for my parents. If I got an A −, they asked why it wasn't an A. I remember when I bragged to my dad that I had learned to ride a two-wheeler—I was so proud! I'll never forget his response. He said, 'Well, it's about time. I thought you'd never get it.' Now I hate it when I see myself being like him in my dealings with my son."

Dean was able to become much more empathic with his son after telling the group how he had felt when he was overly criticized as a child. Children need our guidance, but along with that guidance they also thrive on affirmation. They depend on us to bolster their still-fragile self-esteem. "But how can I tell him he's doing great when he's not?" parents ask me. The key is to separate who your child is from the bad grade or the sloppy room or the missed appointment. When you're overwhelmed by negatives, take a few minutes to think about the positives. Remind yourself, "Terry failed her math test, but today she helped her little brother finish his art project." Remember, too, that your children have identities apart from their specific unacceptable actions. You may not always accept the *actions,* but you can affirm the *person,* wholly and unconditionally.

7

An Unthinkable Rage

Sometimes I'd be so furious that I would clench my fists, leap up and down and bite my knuckles, or I would put my face within a millimeter of theirs and scream bloody murder. . . . If I had never known I could love so fiercely, now I was learning I could feel an almost uncontrollable rage.

—C. W. Smith, *Uncle Dad*

Helen seemed frail and nervous when she began attending my workshop. She admitted that her two-year-old son had been driving her crazy since he was a baby. She revealed that she felt uncomfortable being a mother. "I don't know how to do it. It doesn't come naturally to me," she said in a voice that implied she thought it did for most people. "Andy doesn't seem to be developing like other toddlers. His behavior is so primitive—he's not even talking yet. I blame myself, but I'm angry at him, too, because he just doesn't give me a break. I keep screaming 'What about me?' And sometimes I hit him. I went back to work shortly after he was born, so I think some of the problems are due to my not being home in his first year."

"You blame yourself," I said. "It sounds like you think his problems are your fault."

She nodded and said with urgency, "I say to myself, 'What is a mother?' And you know what I think? I think a mother is a *nothing*. I'm a nothing. I never felt this way when I was working. And now I'm trying to do a job well that I don't even think of as a job. I feel stuck, and we're butting heads. The other day, Andy actually butted me in the face with his head. We're definitely not getting along. And I'm trying so hard. I take him every Tuesday to the park, and I hate it because I'm intimidated by my two-year-old. When I leave the house, I'm so tense I can hardly breathe, because I'm afraid he's going to have one of his frequent tantrums when we get there, and I won't know how to deal with it."

She sighed heavily and stared down at her hands.

"So," Helen said finally, "I'm trying to be this good mother, and I don't know how to find a happy medium, and I don't know how to help my child. It's been tough. I've been taking him to experts—he's obviously different from other two-year-olds—but I don't have an answer. Meanwhile, I have these fantasies of beating him until he stops whining or of taking him to the park and leaving him there. I made a joke to my husband the other day, saying 'We're going to the park, but only one of us is coming back.' "

"How does your husband feel about all of this?" I asked.

Helen laughed. "Oh, he's simply horrified. He just gasps when I say these things and says, 'How could you feel like that?' But I do, I really do. I don't know when this child is going to stop provoking me."

There was silence in the room when Helen had finished speaking. Here was a mother who was experiencing deep pain in her relationship with her son. I was briefly grateful that she had found her way to my class, because clearly if she did not get some help, she might do damage to her child. But I also knew that her problems were too deep to be handled fully here. She needed more help than I could give her. Nevertheless, it might be a start. And I felt the first step was to help her to feel less isolated—less like a monstrous "bad mother"—and more in touch with how normal many of her feelings were.

I sometimes encounter parents whose rage is rooted in a deeply held resentment toward their child. Helen reminded me of Marilyn, a single parent with a seven-year-old daughter, who had joined my class the year before because she couldn't control her rage. "I say terrible things to her," she admitted. "I even swear at her. I resent her so much. I'm all alone, and I have to take care of her and work, and I feel like it's her fault that I have no fun in my life." Marilyn admitted that her vindictive outbursts occurred on a daily basis. She had crossed the line between experiencing the normal parental "brief madness" to being an emotionally abusive parent who needed more sustained, intensive help than my workshop could offer.

However, Marilyn was helped somewhat by being in the class. Group support can be a very powerful aid, especially if one is feeling alone and at wits' end. I was finally able to encourage Marilyn to seek professional help. I believed that would be the best solution for Helen as well, and she eventually took her son to a therapeutic nursery and joined a group of parents with developmentally delayed children. But in the meantime, these mothers had opened up a subject I wanted to explore further with my class.

The topic of uncontrolled parental rage is very much on the public's mind these days. Shocking cases of child abuse fill the newspapers. Sometimes the abuse leads to the death of a child, and we are horrified that such a thing could occur. We wonder; how is this much anger possible? Could I ever lose control like that? It sends chills through us because, on some level, we recognize ourselves in these people. It is one of the things that differentiates those who are parents from those who are not. Before we became parents, we never imagined that anger would be an issue for us. But with parenthood, reality sets in. A colicky baby keeps us awake and exhausted night after night. A defiant three-year-old screams, "You can't make me!" when we try to put her to bed. A seven-year-old responds to our request that he clean up his room by informing us with a snarl, "You're not the boss over me." A teenager curses at us when we set curfews. And suddenly we find ourselves shrieking, slapping, threatening—being consumed by our anger. Many parents have told me that they feel horrified and humiliated when they have scenes with their children in public. They imagine that everyone is watching them and judging them to be bad parents. They're afraid of appearing to be abusive, even when they know they're not. (Children sense this fear and sometimes use it against us, like the child who became angry with his mother and, totally without reason, shouted in a public lobby, "Don't break my arm like the last time!") And yet, many people in my groups can identify with parents who truly are abusive. They are only too conscious of that thin line that separates *wanting* to hurt from actually doing it. And that is a terrible feeling—the fear of losing control with the children we love and are obliged to protect.

It is this conflict of emotions that makes parents so eager to talk about their anger in a safe, nonjudgmental group setting, and to seek advice and input. Today, there are innumerable resources available to help parents learn how to be "better" at raising their children. Entire sections in bookstores are devoted to this pursuit; there are programs

and classes and magazine articles. But ironically, this abun-
dance of information can sometimes feed the panic people
feel when they try to do their best. They learn how a "good,"
loving parent should behave, but receive very little in the
way of practical advice.

"I wonder about this idea many people have that parenting should come naturally," I said to my workshop group.
"Actually, I've met very few parents to whom it did. It
certainly didn't for me!" Parents lay a lot of guilt upon
themselves. We say that if our child is happy, we're good
parents, and if he's not happy, we're miserable parents.
And sometimes it's hard to believe that our kids can elicit
these intense feelings of rage. I asked if any of the other
parents identified with Helen's anger and frustration.

Paula, a pretty young mother of two, was eager to speak.
"When my daughter turned two, she seemed to change
from this sweet, adorable child into a monster. She used
to make my heart sing. Now, especially since the baby was
born, Jenny has become a terror. There have been times
when I've just felt like swatting her across the head when
she acted so obnoxious to me. I can't believe I can feel that
way about her."

"I know what you mean," said Sarah and nodded. "My
four-year-old is impossible sometimes. I don't spank him,
but a few weeks ago I shook him so hard I was scared I'd
really hurt him. Now, I send him to his room when he acts
up because I'm afraid of what I might do if he stays in my
sight another instant."

These feelings of anger are terrifying to parents. We could
never have imagined them when we were thinking about
having children, or while we were pregnant. I believe that
it's important to be able to talk about these frightening
emotions without being judged. It takes courage to face up
to them.

Arlene, whose son was in kindergarten, nodded. "Part of it is that we have such romantic visions of being pregnant and delivering these sweet, angelic babies. It's distressing when the reality turns out to be different. My son was born with allergies, so he was difficult from the start. I was angry about it because nothing was the way I thought it was going to be. It's like getting a present you've been all excited about that turns out completely different from your fantasies. You have to face the disappointment. When my son was two, he was very difficult, but I just had to remind myself that he wasn't doing things just to get me. I also found that distance was absolutely essential. I was around this child twenty-four hours a day, and didn't realize how much I needed to get away from him. When I started using baby-sitters so I could get out and do things for myself, I found a lot of the anger diminished."

When I thought more about it after class, I realized that we had entered different territory that day. While most parents are willing to admit to having tirades, yelling, getting angry, and occasionally spanking their kids, it is a far greater admission to talk about the darker feelings of resentment or even hatred of our children. These are the feelings that can sometimes lead to cruelty and forms of abuse that are terrifying even to consider. But it is important that we address these more severe forms of parental anger because they are very much a reality in our stress-filled society. Abuse may happen when a parent has lost the ability to see any good in a child or is unable to separate feelings from actions. Brenda, one of my students, newly married to a man with a fourteen-year-old daughter, talked about her intense resentment.

"This is the man I want to spend the rest of my life with," she said. "We could be so happy together if it weren't for Joan." Brenda complained that Joan seemed to be doing everything in her power to break up the marriage. "She demonstrates open dislike of me and won't accept any of my friendly overtures. For example, if I ask her if she wants to go shopping, she'll shake her head without answering and go into her room. Whenever I try to tell her about something interesting that has happened, she manages to look excruciatingly bored."

"That sounds like pretty normal fourteen-year-old behavior," I observed.

"I realize that's probably true most of the time," Brenda replied. "But clearly there is antagonism, too, that seems to be related to my new position in the family. Joan does not accept my authority in the house. If I ask her to be home by a certain hour, she deliberately arrives later. When I ask her to do a household chore, she drags her feet and complains so much that it doesn't seem worth it to ask her at all. Worst of all, she often sets up situations that lead to disputes between me and Greg. Recently, I told Greg that I didn't think Joan should be given money for a new skirt she wanted until she had finished cleaning her room— a job I'd been after her to do for several days. He sided with Joan and said he thought I was being too rigid." She looked at me helplessly. "I'm doing my best, but I can't function without support from Greg."

Brenda was also distressed by what she saw as Joan's efforts to sabotage her and Greg's special evenings together. She mentioned one occasion, an eagerly awaited night out for just the two of them that had to be canceled because Joan suddenly developed a stomachache. Brenda was furious, because she believed Joan was being manipulative and had made up the stomachache. But when she voiced her suspicions to Greg, he grew angry and said he was tired of the way she always seemed to see the worst in his daughter.

"Joan is ruining my marriage," Brenda said angrily. "I can see it happening, and I don't know what to do. It sounds so selfish and mean to say that I dislike this girl intensely and resent the way she's interfering with my happiness, but I know things would be much better if she weren't around."

This family had reached the kind of stalemate that is not uncommon in stepparenting situations. They needed to find a way—perhaps with the help of a professional—to step back and view their situation with more objectivity. It might have helped Brenda to know that Joan's resentment was an almost inevitable response to dealing with a stepmother. It wasn't as personal as it seemed. Joan's behavior was a signal that she was hurting and feeling insecure. Greg was fearful of worsening his daughter's pain by appearing to be too harsh, but in the process he was abdicating his parental authority. Brenda was stuck in the middle, feeling attacked from both sides. A professional might have helped them speak openly about and examine the source of their fears and hostility. Brenda might then begin to feel a sense of empathy that she could later summon to remind herself, "Joan is being hateful toward me because she is hurting." Brenda and Joan might never be close, but this family could at least learn to function together.

Even though Brenda was a stepparent, her situation was not unique. Many parents find themselves, for various reasons, reaching a point where they cannot see anything good in a child. These parents wonder how they became so disenchanted with their children, and they struggle to gain back a perspective that will allow them to view their children differently.

Some parents, who would never consider themselves abusive, nevertheless find themselves repeating negative messages to their children without even being aware of how deeply their accusations sting. "You *always* spoil dinnertime for us," a parent might say to a squirmy five-year-old. "There you go again, never satisfied," a parent chides a nine-year-old who asks for a special toy. "Can't you *ever* remember anything?" a parent might shout at a teenager who forgets to pick up an item at the grocery store. The use of absolutes like "always," "never," and "ever" communicate not that the child has done or said something unacceptable, but that *he* or *she* is terminally unacceptable.

Someone once said "Sticks and stones will break your bones, but words will break your heart." It is a reminder that words can sometimes be even more devastating than actions, if children are spoken to with disgust or a constant series of put-downs. Our children *believe* us when we criticize; they are sensitive to the indications we give them that they may be unwanted or unloved:

If only you . . .
If you weren't so . . .
You never . . .
If it weren't for you . . .
You always bug me.
When will you ever learn?
You'll never amount to anything.
I give up—you're hopeless!

Sometimes people find themselves overwhelmed by the daily job of parenting, which can lead to permanently frazzled nerves and exhaustion. Over time, the child becomes the focus of our anger—he or she is the scapegoat who is fully responsible for our bad mood, lack of sleep, messy house, and so on. We find ourselves wondering why we ever decided to have children in the first place. We look ahead, and the years stretch out before us in endless misery.

It is a sad state of affairs, but one which we must use every resource to change—both for our own sakes and the sake of our children.

A Cry for Help

"Some people think hell must be like crying babies," someone once observed. And much as parents may be thrilled to welcome home their little bundle of joy, every parent has experienced those occasions when the crying doesn't end. Most of us have grit our teeth through colic and teething and endless nights when the cries don't stop. But during the past few years, the media have exposed many instances of parents who just snapped in the midst of overwhelming pressure.

What separates a "normal" mother from the one who ultimately expresses her rage and exhaustion by using violent means to make her baby stop crying? We would all like to think that we are far removed from the woman who, at the end of her rope, stopped her baby's crying (and his life) by pushing his face under the water or smothering him with a pillow. But we wonder how different we really are, and we fear the dark urges that may lie dormant, waiting to explode within us. According to an ABC-TV "20/20" report on the subject, "crying babies" is the number-one cause of child abuse in America today. The documentary noted that one in ten babies will not stop crying, regardless of what parents do: singing, rubbing the baby's back, rocking him, walking the floor, feeding, changing—any number of measures designed to soothe. Some babies are capable of crying for hours on end, with seemingly superhuman stamina. These occasions leave parents feeling helpless, resentful, and often filled with hate and rage. As we have said many times, feelings are not the same as actions, but many parents have told me of the terrible guilt they experience when they feel intense negative emotions toward an "innocent, helpless little baby." As one mother said, "I feel like my baby is a black widow spider, and she's sucked all my blood. I'm a shell, and there's nothing left. I'm drained."

Candace, a new mother who was juggling the demands of a full-time job with parenting, said, "It's hard to believe that a tiny baby could have so much power. I'm the adult. I should be in control. But sometimes when he's lying in his crib screaming and screaming, I feel so helpless and so furious at him. The other night I was so tired, and he wouldn't stop crying. I just put my head down on the rim of his crib, and I cried. I had just had it. I looked at him and said, 'Why are you doing this to me?' "

In *Crying Babies, Sleepless Nights*, Sandy Jones suggests that part of the anger mothers feel when babies won't stop crying is due to their belief in what she calls the myth of the perfect mother. "Implicit in the myth," writes Jones, "is the assumption that the mother is responsible for the reactions and behaviors of her baby. . . . If the baby cries, it's her job to stop him. If the baby won't sleep, then it's the mother's task to find a way to *make* him sleep."

Jones refers to a survey in which new mothers were asked how it made them feel when they were unable to quiet their crying babies. Responses included "hostile," "violent," "mildly angry," "exasperated," "underconfident," "hurt at first—then indifferent," "uptight at first—then resigned," "afraid," "worried," "anxious," "unloving," "terrible," "like killing her," "needed," "resentful," "confused," "fed up"—the whole gamut of emotions.

Vicky's one-year-old has begun to teethe, and for several weeks this once-sunny child has been a bundle of tears and screams. Vicky, who has two other children, six and four, and a husband who is often away on business for weeks at a time, complained to my workshop group about feeling completely exhausted and overwhelmed. "I average about four hours sleep a night," she said wearily. "I'm a walking time bomb—stretched to my limit. I never experienced the same difficulties with my two older children, so I wasn't prepared for this. Last week, I reached a breaking point. My husband was home for one night, the first time I had seen him in two weeks. And he was going to be leaving the next day. I prayed that the baby would be quiet. I so needed this time with my husband! But she was up and down every half hour all night, and instead of spending time with my husband, I was walking the floor with this child who couldn't be comforted. I couldn't be comforted either. I sobbed all night, and spoke to my child in an angry, bitter tone of voice. I wondered how long I would be able to handle this. I was afraid of what I might do.

"The next day I called a friend who lived down the block. I was crying. She's an older woman who has raised five children, and I hoped she could give me some advice. She was great. She came right over and ordered me to get out of the house for a few hours. I got in the car and drove to the mall and walked around. After a while, I felt my blood pressure going down. I sat in an outdoor café and slowly ate lunch and relaxed. I thought about my life and about how much I loved my children. I realized that this was a hard period, but it wouldn't last forever. I began, for the first time in weeks, to have loving feelings about my baby. That break saved my life!"

Almost every mother believes that she should be able to cope calmly with the demands of an infant. Anger should be reserved for those who "deserve" it—and how can a little baby deserve our anger? Parents of infants must learn that it's okay to feel angry and resentful. But those feelings should be like warning lights that indicate you need a break before you act out those feelings. Sheila Kitzinger writes sympathetically about the plight of many new parents in her book *The Crying Baby*. "Any mother or father with a constantly crying baby is at risk of being violent to that child. Those who smack, hit or fling a baby on the floor are not monsters. They are human beings at the end of their tether. They have passed the point of endurance and lost control."

Aiming for the Heart

One good reason to be concerned about intense anger toward someone we love is that, when we're enraged, we want to inflict pain or punish. We automatically say the most cutting, hurtful, below-the-belt thing we can think of, and attack the person who is the source of our anger.

Robin told of what happened one day when she was changing Max's diaper and he deliberately kicked her and laughed.

MAX: I kick you!
ROBIN: Please don't kick me. I don't like to be kicked. It hurts me.
MAX (kicking her again): I kick you!
ROBIN (holding his foot still): Kicking hurts me, and if you kick me, I don't want to be with you.

"As I said this, Max kicked me again, this time catching me in the face," Robin related. "I raised my hand to swat him, wanting to hurt him in return—to let him know just how it felt. His eyes seemed to be challenging me to do just that, but I stopped myself. I was furious, though, and so frustrated, because at that moment I felt hateful toward him."

In a poll of one thousand Americans conducted by *Parents* magazine a couple of years ago, 60 percent of the parents surveyed said they thought spanking was okay. As I have said before, I think spanking is at best ineffective and at worst a form of bullying and potential abuse.

Agatha, a woman in my class, spoke angrily about her ten-year-old son. "He's so fresh. Sometimes what he needs is a good whack."

I could see the frustration in her face. "Let's talk about hitting. Agatha, were you hit as a child?"

"Wow! All the time," Agatha replied.

"Try to think back. Do you remember how it felt?"

Agatha frowned. "It was bad. I hated my mother. I was always scared. I guess that's why we don't have a good relationship even now, because I was so afraid of her. I remember too when my brothers were fighting, and she got mad, I'd get scared and run and find someplace to hide because I didn't want to be included in her wrath."

"So the hitting worked in the sense that you were too frightened to be disobedient," I said. "You were scared of getting hit, so there were certain things you didn't do. Do you think you would have been naughtier if your mother had not been a hitter?"

"Maybe so," said Agatha, but she sounded doubtful.

This is one of the reasons some parents believe that hitting works and is justified. But look at the feelings of fear and hate Agatha had toward her mother. "It sounds like even now you haven't forgiven your mother," I said to her.

Agatha nodded. "No, it still makes me mad. And she says I don't spank my son enough—that I spoil him."

"And you agree that what your son needs is to be hit— that it will stop his being fresh."

"I don't know what else to do," she said and sighed.

"Remember your own feelings," I said. "You obeyed out of fear."

A child who obeys out of fear will only do so as long as he or she is scared. A child like this never develops an internalized sense of right and wrong without being policed by a more powerful authority figure.

Dora, the mother of four children ranging in age from seventeen to nine, added, "Also, when your children really need you, they won't come to you if they're afraid of you. They don't see you as being there for them. I need my children to feel they can come to me when they're hurt or upset."

"I realize that," said Agatha. "I would never ask my mother for advice or confide in her because she might get angry and punish me. I remember, once I missed the school bus by accident, and she beat me. So the next time, I didn't tell her. I took a public bus."

I smiled at Agatha. "It may not be what you intended. But you're giving us a very persuasive argument against hitting."

The majority of parents believe, like Agatha, that physical punishment can accomplish positive results. But usually, hitting, slapping, and spanking are punishments that occur when we're at the peak of rage. How many parents hit their children after they've cooled off? I suspect not many. That in itself should be an indication that physical force is an imperfect solution.

We must also consider the role spanking plays in a child's development of conscience. As I suggested to Agatha, a child who is primarily motivated by fear of reprisal cannot independently formulate the conscience that will serve him or her in later years. Selma Fraiberg expressed this idea well in *The Magic Years*, writing that, when parents spank their kids, "The motive for controlling the naughty impulse is a motive that comes from the outside, a fear of external authority and a fear of punishment, and we will find that a conscience that functions on this basis is not a very reliable conscience."

It's really scary when you realize that you *want* to hurt your child. A father in one of my workshops related an incident that had a lasting effect on him. "We were at the dinner table, and I wasn't in a very good mood to begin with, because I'd had a terrible day. My daughter, Tabitha, who is only twelve, told us she had been invited to a party at a boy's house that Friday night. Without stopping to think, I just told her flatly, 'You can't go. You're too young to be going to boys' houses.' At first, she begged me to let her go, giving all the reasons she thought it was okay. She was really getting on my nerves. I was in no mood for this. So I said again in a very loud voice, 'No!' She stood up and pushed her chair so that it tipped over, and yelled, '*God damn you! You're an asshole!*' I was furious—now I understand the expression 'blind with rage.' I stood up and started moving toward her with my hand raised, and she started running toward her room. I chased her down the hall. My wife was screaming in the background for me to stop, but I was too angry. Tabitha had locked the door of her room, and I started pounding and yelling, 'Let me in or I'll break this door down!' I think I really would have. She opened the door, cowering in fear. I grabbed her and shook her hard, then slapped her face. 'Don't you *ever* speak to me that way again,' I said. She was crying hysterically, and by now my wife was hysterical too. I went into the living room and just sat there, my hand tingling. I was too upset to think. Of course, later, I was filled with remorse, and I went to Tabitha's room to try to make up, but she wouldn't speak to me. The next morning, Tabitha left for school early, but when I came down for breakfast, there was a note on my plate."

To Dad,
Last night I was very scared of you. You hurt me inside and you hurt me outside. You hurt me inside because you got so mad at me I thought you didn't love me anymore. I'm sorry for what I said, but I think you should apologize too. I'm still very mad at you in a way, but I still love you very very much. I hope you still love me the same.

from Tabitha

"The note brought tears to my eyes. I felt like such a bully. I had been a bully! I thought about it all day, and the thing that terrified me the most is that I had been unable to control my rage. What if I had seriously hurt her? I couldn't forgive myself. Even though I later apologized, and we made up, I felt that I had established a new undercurrent of fear in the house that hadn't existed there before."

This father did not consider himself to be an abusive man, but he recognized that in this situation, he had behaved abusively. Had the abuse been a pattern, it is unlikely that his daughter would have felt free to write him such a loving note. In households where parents frequently overpower their children to get them to behave, the parents can do lasting damage—even to the point where they create a new generation of potential abusers.

Breaking the Cycle of Abuse

New studies indicate conclusively that children who are abused by their parents—either physically, emotionally, or

sexually—often grow up and become abusive parents themselves. According to John Bradshaw, author of *Bradshaw
On: The Family*, at least ten million people in the United
States were, as children, the victims of violence in their
families. Bradshaw warns that a vicious cycle is set up.
Although every abused child does not grow up to be an
abusive parent (sometimes the reverse happens, and a parent is overly lenient), a recent study by sociologists at Washington University in Saint Louis, suggests that these
formerly abused adults are often poorly functioning men
and women. A study of two hundred adults showed that a
substantial proportion of those suffering from depression
and alcoholism had been harshly and unfairly disciplined
as children. Sociologists Sandra Holmes and Lee Robins
note in *Psychology Today* that "Many of the parental practices found to be deleterious would not qualify as gross
neglect or abuse." But, they conclude, nevertheless, these
practices appear to place kids at risk of mental illness when
they grow up. The most striking fact of the study was the
finding that, in childhood, many of the study subjects lived
in so-called normal homes, demonstrating that abuse can
be present even without accompanying economic or social
factors.

Further studies show that children who are punished
physically lack a quality of empathy and concern that helps
them be caring members of society. In a study of preschoolers who had been physically abused, researchers Mary
Main and Carol George of the University of California at
Berkeley reported in *Developmental Psychology* that the
abused preschoolers not only mirrored their parents' self-
isolation and aggression, but like their parents seemed to
respond almost reflexively to the distress of other children
with fear and anger. For example, the sight and sound of

their peers crying not only aroused no sympathy or concern, it actually provoked reactions ranging from anger to physical attack—including cries of "Cut it out!" hissing, teeth baring, slapping, and even beating the troubled child.

This is a sobering study. Even parents who condone spanking and harsh punishments do not intend to encourage their children to be cruel or without compassion for others. But indeed, this is often the result.

Abusive behavior does not always stem from a state of feeling overwhelmed or being the victim of too much stress. For some parents who have very rigid standards for behavior, harsh punishments are designed only to teach a lesson. And the punishment doesn't necessarily have to be physical to cause harm. According to Anne Cohn, executive director of the National Committee for Prevention of Child Abuse (NCPCA), "Emotional abuse is probably the most heinous form of child abuse. Broken bones mend themselves. Broken spirits don't very easily." A couple of years ago, a California mother received much press attention when she tied her seven-year-old son's hands and sat him in a chair in their front yard. On his face, she fashioned a crudely constructed cardboard pig snout. Around his neck she hung a hand-lettered sign that read "I'm a dumb pig. Ugly is what you will become every time you lie and steal. My hands are tied because I cannot be trusted. This is a lesson to be learned. Look. Laugh. Thief. Stealing. Bad Boy." As the neighbors gathered to stare, tears of shame ran down the young boy's cheeks.

When they read about this, the parents in my workshop were eager to discuss it in class. Without exception, their hearts went out to the small boy forced to endure such a public humiliation. "That's the worst case of abuse I've ever heard of," declared one woman. "If she had taken a belt to him, it could not possibly have been more damaging." Others agreed, and so did the State of California, which brought the mother up on charges of abuse.

The NCPCA receives reports of about 250,000 cases of emotional abuse every year, but they estimate there are many more. Like physical abuse, emotional abuse is often a pattern that is passed down from one generation to the next. Indeed, the mother in the pig-face story claimed that her own mother administered a similar punishment to her when she was a child.

Not every parent is able to cope nonabusively with anger. Parents who were abused themselves as children may need to seek professional help in order to break the cycle. But most parents have times when they wonder if they might be slipping over the line. How do you know if you are? Remember, it is normal to think "I'd like to kill this kid!" It is quite another thing to act out those feelings. As we have noted before, the ability to acknowledge feelings of extreme anger can have the effect of being a pressure valve that lets off some of the steam. If, on the other hand, you often start to hit and cannot stop or rarely experience the relief of pressure; if you wake each morning depressed about spending yet another day in the company of your children; if you cannot find the words to praise but only to blame; if you experience hatred for your children not in an isolated moment but more often than not; if you think your child is bad and unworthy of your loving support, you may need help. These responses go beyond the normal anger that is a part of every parent's experience. In this book, my focus is on the occasional outbursts of anger that the average, loving parent experiences—a form of anger that I believe is inevitable even in the healthiest families. If you have crossed that line, there are many places to go for help. The national hotline for Parents Anonymous is 1-800-421-0353. The line operates from 8:30 A.M. to 5:00 P.M., Pacific Standard Time. If there is no answer, a national 24-hour hotline where parents can call for help is 1-800-448-3000. The hotline is sponsored by Boys Town USA.

8

Mad Is Not Bad

The greatest cruelty that can be inflicted on children is to refuse to let them express their anger and suffering except at the risk of losing their parents' love and affection.

—Alice Miller, *For Your Own Good*

When I was growing up, I quickly learned that the best way to stay out of trouble and please adults was to act agreeable and compliant, even when I didn't feel that way. To argue, disagree, or to reveal intense anger or dissatisfaction was just not acceptable.

My brother was much more open about his hostility, especially with our stepfather, with me, and with his peers. He was frequently in trouble at school and at home as a result of his explosive temper. Observing the consequences of his anger gave me one more good reason to suppress my own. I figured that avoiding expressing anger was the best way to stay out of trouble and to be praised and admired.

My avoidance of anger as a child was not uncommon. As a result of our upbringing and the constant reinforcement of our culture, most of us feel uncomfortable about openly expressing anger, envy, humiliation, or despair. And we are frightened when our children express these emotions.

One of the most difficult things for a parent to do is to acknowledge a child's intense expressions of anger—and to validate that anger as real. When our children are angry, we are tempted to talk them out of their feelings and to make the anger go away as soon as possible:

> Stop making such a fuss. It's not important.
> Can't you be nice?
> Good little girls don't act that way.
> For God's sake, it's not the end of the world.
> You don't really hate your little brother.
> Don't frown!
> In this house, we never say "hate."
> Stop crying, or I'll give you something to cry about!
> You're ungrateful.
> What's wrong with you?
> Don't be a baby.
> You're not really angry—just tired.
> Why do you have to be that way?

Acceptance of angry feelings is a hard lesson to learn—especially for women, who are conditioned from childhood to be the peacemakers of the family. In her groundbreaking book *The Dance of Anger*, Harriet Goldhor Lerner makes this point:

> Women have long been discouraged from the awareness and forthright expression of anger. Sugar and spice are the ingredients from which we are made. We are the nurturers, the soothers, the peacemakers and the steadiers of rocked boats. It is our job to please, protect and placate the world.

The reason we reassure, give advice, offer solutions, and minimize our children's complaints is that we want them to get over their uncomfortable feelings. We love them, and it hurts us to see them unhappy. When we say "Don't worry, it's not so bad, you'll get over it," it's often because we don't want them to be feeling the way they're feeling. We want to make their discomfort disappear.

Jessica, the mother of a two-year-old, related to me how she came to see the importance of giving permission to express anger.

"I was in the kitchen after a hard day at work, breaking apart lettuce for salad. I was tired, and my feet were swollen from the heat, so I leaned on the counter as I worked. Amanda toddled into the kitchen and yelled, 'Don't do dat!' I asked her, 'Do you want to help me make the salad?' But she just kept shouting and repeating the same phrase— 'Don't do dat,' 'Don't do dat.'

"I stopped and just stared at her. Here was this two-foot curly-haired child yelling at me. I thought, what the hell is she so mad about? Her body was rigid, as if something had taken her over. She was filled with rage. I decided to ignore her and continue what I was doing, but then she started pounding me on the thigh. Instead of reacting, I took a deep breath and thought about what to do.

"Then, I don't know why, but I thought about my own mom. She'd never let me yell at her. If I did, she'd beat the shit out of me, and then I'd live in fear all day until Daddy came home. She'd tell him about it, and he'd lecture me for about two hours, telling me how bad I was for acting that way toward my mother. Then, finally, wilted, I'd have to apologize. After all, they were the parents. They were always right. They made all the rules.

"No one ever gave me permission to be angry. My sister, who was four years younger, became my scapegoat. Whenever I hated my parents, I felt I couldn't show it, so I hated my sister. Whenever they yelled at me, I yelled at Marcia, and when they hit me, I ended up hitting her. My folks would intervene every so often. They couldn't understand why I was so evil toward my sister, and neither could I. I was angry at Marcia for the next twenty years, until my therapist gave me permission to get angry.

"I was thinking about all of this, and Amanda was still red-faced and screaming. I gave her total space to act out her anger. I was filled with tears at the revelation of the deprivation I had felt as a child, and how much I had needed this same space. God, it felt so *good* to give it to her. I didn't even know where her anger came from. But I gave her permission to express it.

"Finally, she stopped, exhausted. Her limp, sweet little body embraced me, and she buried her face in my thighs and said, 'I love you.' I bent down, took her in my arms, and said, 'I love you, too, Amanda.' And we stood in the kitchen for a long time, just holding each other.

"Then she skipped out of the room."

I found this to be a poignant story, certainly not because I recommend that children be allowed to kick and hit when angry, but because it demonstrates such a great break-through in Jessica's self-awareness. Once she recognized that anger was not a bad emotion but a normal one, and one that she was never allowed to express as a child, she felt freer allowing Amanda to let out her intense irrational feelings without judging her bad, as she herself had been judged as a child.

Many parents who answered the survey questions expressed their own discomfort with anger.

I had Victorian parents. They didn't tolerate anger or disrespect. I was not permitted to be angry. Thus, when my son expresses anger, I feel threatened by his sassiness, willfulness, and obnoxiousness. It's behavior I have trouble allowing myself, and that's why I'm threatened.

I'd walk ten miles to avoid anger. I grew up in a family where we weren't allowed to express anger.

I always thought the perfect parent was the one who didn't get angry. Her voice tone was low and well-modulated. She was in control. I hate myself when I hear the high-pitched screaming sound coming from my mouth.

It upsets me when my child is angry, because I feel I'm doing something wrong. I want him to be happy, and when a person is angry, he's not happy.

We have so little time to spend together as a family. I hate to see it wasted with negative emotions.

I always learned that if you loved someone, you were kind and tried to be understanding of that person. When I'm angry, I feel it isn't my "better self."

When I was growing up, I always felt that my emotions were squelched, so I determined to let my daughter fully express herself. Now sometimes I think I went too far the other way because she expresses herself so much!

My son is so volatile and explosive that I find myself walking on eggshells so he won't blow up. His anger is scary to me.

Once we accept our children's anger as normal, we can look for ways to acknowledge it and allow them to resolve their problems. The good news is that once we validate a child's anger, we can help him dissipate it and move on.

Gladys, one of my workshop students, found this to be true, as she relates in this story about her son, Cecil.

"I promised I'd buy my four-year-old son, Cecil, the Thundercat toy. He's been asking for it for months. The toy store said it would come in Tuesday, and Cecil counted the days. But when we went to the store on Tuesday, they said it hadn't yet come in. Cecil hid his head in my skirt and cried silently. As we left the store, the full force of his disappointment hit him, and his sobs grew louder."

GLADYS: I can see how disappointed you are.

CECIL (angry now): They have no right to do that! To break a promise to a kid!

GLADYS: I know. It's a bummer.

CECIL (furious, no longer crying): I want to kill them. I'm going to kill them.

GLADYS: Wow! You're so angry you wish you could kill those people in the store.

CECIL: Yes. Next time I see them I'm going to.

GLADYS: How do you plan on doing it?

CECIL: I'm going to call on Superman to help me.

GLADYS: How does Superman kill people?

CECIL: He doesn't. But I have a good connection with Superman, and he'll do what I say. Well, maybe he won't kill them, but he sure will be angry!

This parent allowed her son to use his fantasy as a safe outlet for his anger. When a child starts talking about killing people, like Cecil did, many parents might respond, "Don't say that. That's a terrible thing to say," and worry about their child's violent feelings. Instead, Gladys held back and let Cecil mentally play out the scene, recognizing that *words and feelings are not the same as actions.* And she discovered that when she allowed Cecil to fantasize, his anger gradually diminished.

Children's minds are rich receptacles of fantasy, and their angry expressions often reflect imagination that is beyond our sober adult comprehension. But playing along with the fantasy can sometimes bring a child out of his fury. One mother handled a difficult situation by voicing a fantasy of her own.

"I was getting my five-year-old son ready to go to school, along with my two-year-old, and I announced that this morning we were walking," Jane recalled. "Matt hates to walk, and he began to whine insistently about taking the bus."

MATT: I'm not walking. I want to take the bus.

JANE: It's too hard today with the baby in the stroller. Today we have to walk.

MATT (really whining): No, no, I'm tired. I want to take the bus.

JANE: Matt, I'm warning you.

MATT: My feet hurt!

[Jane started to yell, then took a deep breath and let a couple of minutes pass.]

JANE: I'm getting so furious with you that in one more minute my eyes are going to pop out of my head and roll down Broadway all the way to Canal Street!

[Matt started to giggle, and the crisis passed.]

Gladys and Jane found solutions that worked well, but parents often complain to me that these techniques don't always work. And if by "work," they mean that merely acknowledging feelings will make children "snap out of it" and be happy, they're right. There are no miraculous responses that will make intense feelings of fear, rage, sadness,

and jealousy just disappear in a cloud of smoke. We discussed parents' frustrations with the way kids express their
strong feelings one morning in my workshop.

"I'm patient up to a point, but I feel angry rather than
empathetic when my son, Gerald, doesn't get over being
upset," said Jackie, whose son was a rowdy eight-year-old.
"I start out being supportive, but when he doesn't stop,
then I get annoyed."

Rebecca, the mother of a six-year-old, agreed. "Yes, I
find with Vanessa that it doesn't always short-circuit it when
I say 'Oh, you're sad' or 'I see that you're angry.' Sometimes,
it fuels her anger, like she's looking for more. Then I say
to myself, 'How much more can I give?' "

"Yes, this is frustrating," I agreed. "Especially when you
have recognized the validity of your child's reactions, and
it still doesn't seem to diminish his anger, or he's still
pushing your buttons."

"With me, it's not that so much," said Rebecca. "It's
that my daughter's actions are so inappropriate. It's enough
already. And I guess I think that if I were more effective,
she'd stop complaining and be happy."

Of course, it would be so much easier if we had a magic
formula to turn our children's complaining and whining
into smiles and hoots of joy. It's hard for parents to shake
the idea that anger is a negative thing to be gotten rid of
as quickly as possible. Our most important role as parents
is not to get kids *over* their strong emotions, but to help
them feel that we understand and accept them. To do this,
we must be skillful at describing the feelings or acknowledging as specifically as possible what the child is saying.
We're not always going to feel empathetic, so we might be
saying "I understand" but communicating something quite
different with our tone of voice. The best thing in that
case is to be authentic. Rebecca might say "I hear how

upset you are, but I can't listen anymore. I'm getting impatient."

The goal is to help our children find acceptable ways to express anger. But the first step is to acknowledge what the child is feeling. At that moment, he or she is really upset. It doesn't help to say "You shouldn't be upset—this isn't worth being upset about." Our children have a right to feel angry, just as we do.

The Risk of Anger

According to Violet Oaklander, Ph.D., in her audiotape "Working with the Anger of Children and Adolescents," anger is the most misunderstood of all emotions. Oaklander notes that anger has a bad press because so many of us were taught that it was bad and that we should avoid it at all costs. Children, she says, learn very young that anger is dangerous, and therefore they do not learn healthy, appropriate ways to express what is a normal human emotion. "The child thrives on acceptance, approval, love," Oaklander explains.

> At an early age, when he is still fairly congruent, he may express angry feelings toward his mother, for which he may meet disapproval, rejection, and what feels to be a loss of love. He begins to learn that the expression of angry feelings is full of danger to himself, and he must do whatever he can to avoid further injury. Since anger is unavoidable, he must make some determination about what to do when he feels it. He usually tries to push the feeling down, to keep it in. But the unexpressed emotion lies within the child like a rock, interfering with healthful growth.

When I find my students struggling to accept their own and their children's feelings of anger, I have them do an exercise which helps them remember how it was when they were children. I tell them to take a sheet of paper and write down some of the ways their parents responded when they showed their anger or disappointment. I remember how Enid, a mother in my class, experienced a breakthrough when she reviewed her list, which included these points:

1. I got the silent treatment. She would refuse to talk to me (sometimes for days) as punishment. Also, she'd get my father to stop talking to me.
2. She always made me apologize to *her* when we had a fight—even when I thought she was wrong. She would never admit she was wrong.
3. She never let me express anger to my brother. When I said "I hate you" to my brother, she would come along and say "Don't say that, you don't really mean it, he's your only brother, you don't really hate him. . . ." She always denied my anger.

After Enid read her list, she looked up at me with wide eyes. "My mother was afraid of anger," she said softly. "But when she wasn't speaking to me, I could *feel* her anger. It was like a cauldron boiling beneath the surface. I learned from her that, when you are angry, you mustn't show it. You keep it to yourself. If you express it, that's bad. When I think back, though, I remember wishing desperately that my mother would yell at me and get it over with, instead of imposing that dreadful silence."

Betty, the mother of a ten-year-old boy, struck a responsive chord in my workshop group when she said one day, "I give in a lot because I am afraid of Josh. Afraid of his anger and hostility."

"Tell us more about this, Betty," I prodded, sensing this was an important, usually unspoken, issue.

She spoke slowly, searching for words. "I guess I worry that, when he really gets mad, I can't do anything to control it."

"And what might happen if you can't control it?"

"I don't know."

"Will he hurt himself? Hurt you? Break something?"

She shook her head. "I see that I've never thought about it specifically. I guess I'm afraid that if I take a firm stand and say no, he'll just get crazy and out of control. I'm beginning to realize, though, that I'm allowing him too much power, and it causes me to give in too easily. Maybe what I'm really afraid of is that he'll hate me."

No parent is comfortable watching a child losing it, and we have to stop them from hurting themselves or us. Children have moments when they really do hate us, but we can't allow that to stop us from setting limits, no matter how mad they get. It helps if we don't automatically assume that a child's angry response proves that there is something wrong with us."

I encouraged Betty to take a firm stand with what she considered to be nonnegotiable issues. "You can expect to be tested," I assured her. "But try not to let his extreme behavior make you back down. It won't always work—that is, it won't prevent your son from being upset and challenging you. But the alternative is to abdicate your role as parent."

Finding Acceptable Ways
to Express Anger

Even parents who think they are dealing wisely with their
children's anger, wish they could offer them more acceptable options. Helping our children discover appropriate
ways to express their disappointment and rage is a hard—
but necessary—lesson to learn. Julius Segal, Ph.D., notes
in his paper "Children and Anger: Family Matters," published for the International Conference on Children and
the Media (Washington, D.C., 1988),

> Although we are all born with the capacity for anger, the
> manner in which children *express* the emotion—what they
> end up *doing* with it—depends heavily on learning. How our
> young learn to deal with and manifest anger can resound for
> a lifetime. The emotional and physical price for misgoverning
> this basic emotion is heavy—paid in poor mental health and
> physical health, flawed relationships, damaged careers, and
> wounded families. As Aristotle said, "Anyone can become
> angry—that is easy, but to be angry with the right person, to
> the right degree, at the right time, for the right purpose, and
> the right way—that is not easy."

I give parents in my workshops an exercise where I ask
"How do your kids express their anger?" They have little
trouble finding examples, which I write on the blackboard:

Sticking out their tongues
Swearing and name calling
Spitting
Crying
Yelling "Shut up!"

Saying "I hate you!"
Hitting
Biting
Kicking
Throwing tantrums
Going limp
Defying me
Throwing things
Sulking
Whining
Acting fresh or sarcastic
Slamming doors

"Do you agree that some expressions are more acceptable than others?" I ask.

They nod their heads in agreement.

"So, do you also agree that it is not anger itself that is the problem, but some of the ways it is expressed?"

They agree with that, too. Then I ask "What do you think are acceptable ways to express anger and what are not?" I write these answers in two columns on the board:

Acceptable	*Not Acceptable*
Crying	Destroying property
Going outside to sulk	Using four-letter words
Punching a pillow	Hitting, kicking, punching, biting
Saying angry words	Name calling
Hitting the "bop bag"	Spitting
Yelling "I'm mad!"	Disobeying
Isolating themselves	
Making an ugly face	
Writing an angry note	
Pounding clay	
Shredding paper	

We then study the lists and talk about acceptable versus unacceptable forms of anger. Each family has its own rules for what is and is not allowed in the household. But it's best to offer alternatives, so children understand that there are some outlets for their anger—that they don't have to keep it bottled up inside. For example, a parent might say "No hitting. Use words." Or "No throwing things in the house—only in the yard." Or "No swearing in front of Mom—only swear in your room." Or "Spitting is okay, but only in the sink." One parent in my workshop has an angry corner in her son's room, where he can pound pillows or punch his clown, whom he has named "Mr. Stupid Face."

When we have finished discussing the lists on the board, I say to the parents, "Now tell me what you consider acceptable anger for yourself."

There is usually some uncomfortable shuffling in the room, since parents have such a struggle admitting that their anger is acceptable under any circumstances. Once when I was doing this exercise, the tension was broken when a mild-mannered young woman spoke up from the back of the room: "I throw plates against the wall."

Everyone howled at the picture—this woman was always so quiet and soft-spoken. When the laughter died down, I nodded and said, "That's your idea of acceptable anger."

She shrugged. "They're only plates."

"Yes—what are some others?" We put a list up on the board, which includes the following:

Grimace
Growl
Swear in a foreign language
Get on the Exercycle and pedal madly
Wash dishes, scrub, clean

Call a friend
Slam doors
Pound the pillows
Leave the room
Go for a walk or a run
Say "I'm really mad!"
Play music loudly
Go into the bedroom and scream
Breathe deeply
Raid the refrigerator

Reviewing the list, I said, "Look at all the new possibilities you have for venting your anger." And several parents told me later that it was a very helpful exercise. Not only did it affirm anger as being okay, it also gave them options for how to express it.

Many parents can't abide hearing their children "talk fresh." Indeed, it's startling to hear the repertoire of ugly words that can tumble out of these small mouths. We certainly need to discourage rude or offensive words, but at the same time we need to help our children find acceptable alternatives. Ann, whose twelve-year-old often gets very sassy when he is angry, tried to help him find a new way of expressing his feelings. "David is a very creative, articulate child, so the last time he became angry and spoke in a fresh way, I told him firmly, 'I can't listen to this kind of talk right now. Your words are too offensive and insulting, and I don't want to hear them. Why don't you write down what's bothering you, and I'll read what you have to say.' Then I closed the door of my room, shutting him out. He wasn't happy about it. I could hear him pounding around in his room for a while. But then things grew very quiet. About a half hour later, a sheet of paper came sliding under my door. It read:

Dear Mom,

You and I disagree on many things. I try to be helpful but I do not enjoy your turning off the TV during my programs all the time and telling me to clean my room while I'm trying to watch. What if I turned the television off while you were watching 'Dynasty'? You wouldn't be all smiles. As for home-work, I finished it before TV. Hebrew is hard, but I've worked on it quite a bit. I do good in school and I think you should be proud. You know I do my homework. Also, a few days ago I did clean up my room and put my clothes away.

    You hurt me tonight and I don't think that I should be the only one to apologize, although I might be wrong. If you want to talk to me, then do so but take my thoughts into con-sideration.

Your son,
David

"I was delighted with this letter," said Ann proudly. "It was such a simple, clear articulation of his point. I was able to respond directly to his complaints, because he told me what was wrong, instead of calling me names."

Love is complicated—and we love our children a lot. We would do anything for them. We want them to be happy. But we don't always *feel loving,* and I believe that's okay. Children don't always feel loving toward us either. I think it's helpful to let a child know, when she has delib-erately misbehaved or defied us, that we are not feeling very loving at that moment. Our anger at our children is inevitable and often justified. But it needs to be separate from what we feel about them as people.

Child-raising expert Fitzhugh Dodson, Ph.D., advises in *Experts Advise Parents,*

Children often fear their own anger because they feel guilty about the intensity of their negative feelings toward people they care about. They hold their anger inside because they're afraid that their parents would stop loving them if they were aware of the strength of their feelings. Children need to understand that love and anger are not opposites. They are both signs of caring.

According to the Institute for Mental Health Initiatives (IMHI) in Washington, D.C., anger can lead to positive action. It is a signal that something isn't right—and the power of the angry emotion can serve as a catalyst for bringing about change. If we can begin to use our anger as a tool to learn more about our own and our children's deeply felt needs, we can transform the bitter feuds into springboards for growth. Admittedly, this is not easy to do, since our attitudes about anger are so deeply imbedded. It requires that we learn ways to step back from the immediate force of our rage, acknowledge it, and then respond without being hurtful. The following chapter suggests techniques for doing that.

9

Eight Weapons in the War on Anger

The best time to give swimming lessons is not when someone is drowning.
                                        —Dr. Haim Ginott

There's a saying that goes "Dance, don't wrestle," and this admonition speaks to the way family conflicts are best resolved. If our response is to win by force, we cannot hope to reach a peaceful solution. When we inflict our wills at the expense of theirs, we are simply being bullies, and although we might win the battle, we're eventually going to lose the war.

Many parents have expressed confusion about this. They don't want to bully their children, but sometimes being punitive seems to be the only way to handle a situation. They see only two options: Being a strong, authoritarian, "because I say so" parent who is in control, or being a wimpy, permissive parent who always lets the child win.

Rather, you can find a middle ground for handling confrontations—like learning the steps to a dance. These are the practical methods of action and response that we discuss in my workshops. The following are eight guidelines that, if followed, are capable of bringing relative peace to your household battlefield.

1. EXIT OR WAIT

It is possible to act a little nicer than you feel, but not much. For this reason, the two most important four-letter words to remember when you are angry are *exit* and *wait*. When we are so incensed that we're about to lose control, exiting or calling time out can give us a breather so that we're not at the mercy of our "short madness." Attacks that occur in the heat of anger are usually met with reactive anger.

In an angry moment, silence, or a brief withdrawal, is sometimes the safest answer. The wonderful thing about saying nothing is that you never have to take it back. Parents are often reluctant to try this. As one mother said, "If I leave the room, won't he think he's won?" On the contrary, exiting can be a quiet, powerful way of demonstrating just how serious you think the situation is, as well as modeling self-control. Gail, whose eight-year-old was reacting angrily to her command that he turn off the TV and do his homework, demonstrated as much in the following dialogue:

GAIL: I've told you three times. Now, turn it off!
JOHN (whining): Oh, Mom, come on!
GAIL: Now!
JOHN: No. I won't! You can't make me.

Gail marches over and turns the television off. John jumps up, furious, and pushes her away from the set. Then he turns it back on. Gail feels overcome by fury. She raises her hand, then stops herself.

GAIL (very firmly, anger in her voice): I am so furious with
   you right now that I am walking out of this room.
[She strides out, closing the door to the playroom. From
   the kitchen she hears silence. The TV has been turned
   off. Fifteen minutes later, John comes into the kitchen.]
JOHN: Mom, I'm doing my homework.
GAIL: Good.
JOHN: I feel bad that I pushed you. I wanted to watch that
   program so much.
GAIL: Pushing is never allowed, no matter how mad you
   get.
JOHN: I know. I just got so mad. I won't do it again. I'm
   really sorry, Mom.
GAIL: Okay. I accept your apology, and I appreciate it. After
   you finish your homework, you can watch TV.

If Gail had slapped John, it would have been hard for
her to make the point convincingly that hitting and pushing
are not allowed in their household. She chose to *exit* and
wait until she had cooled down—allowing John to cool
down too.

Some parents have expressed the concern that leaving
the room or waiting to respond makes it appear that they
are giving in. But by stating firmly why she was leaving the
room, Gail left no doubt in her son's mind that he had
pushed her too far. Few children would see this as a victory.

It is important, when adults take time out, that they
make it clear they're exercising self-control, not abdicating
authority. They should also indicate what they expect the
child to do to make amends.

2. "I," NOT "YOU"

When a child does something to make us angry, our automatic response may be to shout an accusation: "Why are

you behaving like such a brat?" "What kind of a slob are you—throwing your jacket on the floor?" "You are impossible!" The message we communicate is that the child is unacceptable, not the action. "You" statements have the ability to wound. "I" statements make the point much more effectively, without damaging a child's self-esteem. When you're angry, it's better to say (or even shout) "I'm mad," not "You're bad." For instance, "I am very angry that you tore your new dress," instead of "What a pig you are, always ruining your nice clothes. Do you think money grows on trees?" State how you feel, rather than make a declaration about the child's character.

Here are some examples of "I" statements:

I need quiet right now.
I can't concentrate on my driving with this noise.
I feel too tired to listen.
I am furious that you broke our rule.
I am very angry!
I want to be left alone right now.
I don't like it when you call me that name.
I won't be spoken to like that.
I'm not available for aggravation.

3. **STAY IN THE PRESENT**
Don't use the incident as a springboard for gloomy forecasts or as an opportunity to dredge up ancient history. Say "I'm disappointed in this report card," not "Your report cards are always bad" or "At this rate, you'll never amount to anything." Futurizing is a common reaction to children's misbehavior. Stick to the present and banish such dire predictions as "You'll end up in jail like Uncle Archibald—a miser, spendthrift, lazy bum. . . ." and so on.

In spite of her frustration, the mother in the following

incident fought—and won!—the battle to stay focused on the issue at hand, even though she was tempted to make broad accusations.

"Recently I was called to school by my ten-year-old son's teacher," Aurora related. "She showed me his math papers and said he was failing. I left the conference very angry with Lowell, because he had never indicated to me that he was having trouble. He has told me that he wants to take responsibility for his own schoolwork, and he doesn't want me interfering. But look what happened when I let him have some independence!

"The drive from the school to our house is five minutes, but I stretched the drive out, because I knew I needed time for my anger to cool. When I finally arrived home, I was greeted at the door by a smiling, seemingly happy Lowell.

LOWELL: Hi, Mom. How was your day?

AURORA: Fine, Lowell, except for the conference I just had with Miss Smith.

LOWELL (head tilted down): Oh.

AURORA (waiting a few minutes, then speaking): Lowell, did we make a deal that I won't bug you about your schoolwork unless you feel you need or want my help?

LOWELL: Yes, Mom.

AURORA: What happened to our deal?

LOWELL: What do you mean?

AURORA (staying calm and objective): Miss Smith gave me these papers, which show you have failed all your math assignments. I don't think our deal is working, because you never told me that you needed help. I don't think you want to fail math, but leaving this up to you hasn't worked. So what do you think we should do now?

LOWELL (with tears in his eyes): I'm sorry, Mom. I knew I was falling behind, but I didn't want to tell you I failed on these assignments. I was afraid you wouldn't let me go to Little League.

AURORA: Lowell, you didn't give me a chance to help you. You agreed to let me help you if you had trouble, and I agreed not to butt in. If you want me to give you responsibility for your work, you have to keep your word when we make an agreement.

LOWELL: I'll try. Are you very mad at me?

AURORA: I'm disappointed and concerned. But I'm willing to figure out a solution, if you are. Miss Smith suggested that you write down and complete the problems that you have wrong. If you want my help, ask. I'll look at it when it's finished.

LOWELL (relaxing): Okay, Mom.

AURORA: When will you have this completed?

LOWELL: In two days.

"Then Lowell came over and hugged me. Later that evening, we spoke about the agreement. I told Lowell that I felt we had to change it a little bit. I suggested that every Friday he bring all his papers for me to see, and in the meantime I would not bug him."

After the conference with the teacher, Aurora was angry and disappointed. She knew Lowell found it hard to get good grades unless he studied very hard. She was afraid that if things didn't improve, he wouldn't be eligible for the junior high school she wanted him to attend. Aurora also felt a bit betrayed because Lowell had broken their agreement, and she wasn't sure she could trust him in the future. Instead of voicing these larger fears and threatening Lowell with the terrible consequences she imagined for his future schooling, she stuck to the issue at hand and renegotiated the agreement to address the problem specifically. She didn't say—and it must have been tempting—that there would be dire consequences if Lowell broke the contract again. In spite of his failure to keep the agreement, Aurora was considerate of Lowell's dignity. She gave him another chance. Her restraint made it impossible for Lowell to get angrier at her than at himself, so he was more amenable to finding a solution.

Avoid lengthy tirades that become an accumulation of other grievances. State your point—"I'm furious about the way this room looks"—and stop. What sometimes happens with rage is the "last straw" reaction. Incidents have been piling up and you've restrained yourself, but then one more little thing happens, and you lose control. That's when you can't resist the tendency to get carried away, listing all the things that your child has done that day or week or month. One parent described a scene where she blew her top when she found her son had been using her brand-new computer—which he knew he was not allowed to do. When she saw him, she shouted at him to stop and told him how angry she was. But in the process, she also mentioned that he

had messed up the living room
forgotten to put the cap on the toothpaste
left the milk out of the refrigerator
not put his clothes in the hamper
failed to feed the dog
not turned the TV off when he left the room

By the end of this tirade, her child was understandably overwhelmed. Most kids simply turn off their hearing after the first sentence, becoming what I call "mother deaf." If you speak with brevity and authority, the message has a better chance of hitting home.

4. AVOID PHYSICAL FORCE AND THREATS

If spanking worked, we'd only have to do it once. And when you've won by asserting physical power as a big person over a small person, you've won nothing.

Try not to threaten or punish when you're in the midst of a rage. Unreasonable threats, stinging words, and hitting rarely happen when we are calm. We usually end up making threats that are unenforceable—"You're grounded for life" . . . "No TV for a month"—and the physical punishments and harsh words are demeaning.

Some parents use the threat of physical violence, and find that it can be just as traumatic as the violence itself. Erin tells about driving in the car with her eight-year-old daughter, who had been giving her a hard time all afternoon.

MOM: Okay, Carol, I'm sick and tired of this back talk! I don't want to be treated like you've been treating me. I don't deserve it. I have feelings too. I'm not just a mom—I'm a person.

CAROL: Mom! Don't yell at me.

MOM (voice rising): I'm not yelling. You're the one who has been yelling at me all afternoon.

[Carol mimics Erin's words in a singsong way, which makes Erin angrier.]

MOM: You stop that right now or you're going to get a spanking you won't forget!

CAROL (starting to cry): You're always telling me hitting isn't allowed. Anyway, if you can hit me, why can't I hit you back?

MOM (calming down): You're right. We don't hit. I'm sorry.

CAROL (sobbing): But you said it! You said you would spank me.

MOM: I was angry. I won't spank you. I don't spank.
CAROL (after a few moments): Mommy, I'm sorry too. I need a hug.
[Erin pulls the car into a shopping center lot and stops. She reaches over and gives Carol a big hug and kiss.]

Erin later reflected about the incident. "I threatened physical violence as a means of altering Carol's behavior, even though I wasn't planning to follow through. It was not a productive measure. It is difficult when those 'pushed to the limit' moments occur not to revert to behaving the way my parents did. And I hated them when they used to threaten and scream and spank me. I tend to repeat those old techniques when my daughter gets fresh, even though they never worked for me when I was a kid. I either got more defiant or I withdrew. If I hadn't been so mad, I wouldn't have threatened to hit her when I don't even believe in parents hitting."

5. STAY SHORT AND TO THE POINT

Dana, whose son, Dean, always objected when it was time for him to take his bath, dreaded the inevitable confrontations. Usually, they ended up with her dragging a screaming Dean into the bathroom, yelling "Why do you always have to give me so much trouble?" She tried a more direct, firmer approach:

DANA: Time for your bath. Do you want bubbles tonight or just plain water?
DEAN: I don't want a bath!
DANA: It's time for your bath. [Leads him into the bathroom.] Guess what?
DEAN (momentarily distracted): What?

DANA: After your bath, we can read the new book we bought today.

DEAN: I want to read it now.

DANA (firmly): First bath, then story.

Beware of long explanations. When a child asks "Why can't I?" instead of giving him a long lecture that he's heard many times before, you might ask "Why do you think?" Or use humor. Say "Do you want my two-minute explanation or my twenty-minute explanation?" As the saying goes, "Never wrestle with a pig. You'll just get muddy—and the pig likes it." Kids have endless time to play point-counterpoint, in an effort to wear you down. I know many parents whose children are ready for law school by age five! They are the ones whose parents often overdo reasoning and explaining, in the hopes that if only they give their children enough explanations, the kids will stop wanting what they wanted in the first place. Don't be afraid to sound like a broken record, briefly but firmly repeating your instruction:

No boots in the kitchen.
Cookies are for after dinner.
No hitting.
Socks belong in the hamper.
Homework before TV.
One treat is enough.
We're shopping for food, not for toys.
Time for bed.
After eight o'clock, it's grown-up time.

Be specific. It's pointless to tell a five-year-old to clean up her room. If you expect results, you might wait forever. Saying "Clean up your room" is much too vague. Children need specific instructions—although not too many. For instance, you might say "The beads belong in the bead box. The pj's on the floor belong in the hamper. The books belong on the shelf by your bed. We rinse the plates before putting them in the dishwasher." Maybe you can make it into a game, since young children love to play and think that cleaning up is a chore. Say "I'll bet you can't do those three things before the timer rings." If you make it a race or help them, they are usually more amenable. Also, make sure you give them a system that makes cleanup easier—such as hooks at child's level, low shelves for books, clear boxes marked with the pieces they should contain, and so on.

Sometimes one word can communicate everything you want to say:

Walk. (Stop running.)
Boots. Jacket. Hat. (Put on your . . .)
Teeth. (Brush . . .)
Door. (Close the . . .)
Socks. (Pick up the . . .)
Coat. (Hang up your . . .)

6. PUT IT IN WRITING

A written message can be an effective and calming way to express your feelings in a manner others can understand. Writing is good for several reasons—one being that it is a naturally calming activity. It's hard to maintain rage in the course of getting a piece of paper, finding a pen, sitting down, and forming the words in your head. Here are some good examples of effective letter writing.

In the first example, Mom had noticed that her daughter, Kerry, had crossed the street without taking adequate precautions. She was concerned about her carelessness, but rather than confront Kerry directly the minute she walked in the door, she left this note.

Dear Kerry,
Crossing streets is dangerous. I love you and I don't want you hurt. I have to know you will follow my rules, so that I won't worry when you walk home from school.

Today there were two rules you didn't follow, and that scares me.

1. You waited to cross *in* the street, instead of on the curb.
2. You crossed against the light.

If you can't follow these rules, I cannot allow you to walk home alone. Please think about this and RSVP.

Love,
Mom

Later, Kerry acknowledged the note, and promised that she would be more careful. They spent a few minutes talking about ways she could remember to cross the street safely, and reviewed the rules together one more time.

In the second example, the superintendent of their apartment building reported to Al's mother that her son had been very fresh when asked not to play in a certain area around the building. At first, she was furious at Al's rude behavior and was about to scream at him and threaten to take away his Nintendo for good. After she cooled off, she wrote the following instead:

Dear Al,
It has been brought to my attention that George, the super, saw you and Roger playing ball in the hallway yesterday, and that when he asked you to stop, you gave him a rude answer.

This note is a *reminder*.

Dad and I are very proud to have a son like you, and we expect you to answer George in a polite and respectful manner.

If there is a problem or you disagree with him, come and see
Dad or me immediately.

Thank you. I love you.

Mom

After receiving this note, Al apologized to both the super
and to his mother. He did not become defensive because,
instead of attacking him, his mother had reiterated her
values and expectations, and expressed her trust that he
could do better. She was descriptive, and avoided accusations and blame.

When you put your thoughts in writing, you also allow
yourself a cooling-down period—it is another way of exiting
and waiting. It helps to establish distance, privacy, and
time to reflect. It can also open the door to a new closeness
and mutual understanding—as is demonstrated in this third
example.

Lee often told my workshop group of the bitter fights her
ten-year-old daughter, Kyla, had with her father. Robert
was an older father of fifty, who had adult children by a
first marriage. Lee, who is fifteen years his junior, speculated
that the confrontations might be caused by Robert's more
traditional parenting style—the one he had used with his
children twenty years ago. "Kyla resents the way he lays
down the law," she said, "and she is very aware of the fact
that her father is much older than her friends' fathers. Fifty
isn't that old, of course, but to a child I suppose it seems
ancient. I also suspect that it worries Kyla that her father
is older, and that might be the source of some of the tension.
One day I heard her girlfriend ask Kyla if her father was
going to die soon. I couldn't hear her response, but I wonder
if she does worry about it."

Lee was an exceptionally sensitive and wise woman, with
an ability to see beyond the superficial issues. One day, she

reported the following incident to the workshop group. Robert and Kyla had had a particularly hostile confrontation, with much screaming and threatening. Kyla was angry because she said Robert was too bossy when they played sports. Robert was hurt because he felt Kyla didn't appreciate the time he spent with her. After the fight, Kyla ran crying to her room. When Lee went in to check on her later, her daughter told her that she felt very upset about what happened, but she was afraid to say anything because her father was so mad. Lee made a gentle suggestion. "Why don't you write your dad a note and tell him how you feel."

Later, Robert showed Lee the note Kyla had slipped under his briefcase. It read:

Dear Dad,
I'm sorry. Will you forgive me and next time pleas on a weekend don't boss me!!! Because sometimes you can be a real pain. When people get mad they say things they don't mean so don't take it searously. Ok!!!

Love,
Kyla

Robert was clearly moved by his daughter's note. "I love her so much," he told Lee. "I don't understand why we have so many fights. She seems to be so upset with me."

"Maybe her anger isn't always about what it seems," suggested Lee mildly. "You know, you're older than her friends' fathers, and deep down, she might be afraid that you'll get sick and die, and she'll lose you."

Robert had never considered that before. After giving it much thought, he sat down and wrote back to Kyla.

Dear Kyla,
Thank you for your card. I don't mean to boss you on week-

ends. I realize you resent it when I try to correct your tennis swing.

But remember, I have a lot of experience coaching sports. I will sometimes make suggestions on how you can improve and get more pleasure out of sports. You don't have to follow my suggestions, but please listen politely.

Please don't worry about my being older than other fathers. Remember, I am young in spirit and am feeling fine and healthy. I hope to be around to take care of you and be with you for many years. I don't expect that I will be old and feeble for many, many years.

I'm sorry we had a fight. Let's try to stay calmer in the future. I'll try not to yell at you. You try to listen to me, even if you don't agree.

All my love,
Dad

Even though angry confrontations cannot be avoided completely, most parents strive to break through the anger and find a meaningful reconciliation. Restoring good feelings in the aftermath of an angry confrontation is essential. With Lee's help, Robert and Kyla found a way to heal the rift in their relationship and reach a new understanding that might make a difference in the way they communicate with one another in the future.

7. FOCUS ON THE ESSENTIAL

In parent groups we talk a lot about making rules and fights that break out when these rules get broken or are ignored. Parents have to decide for themselves what is really important in their households. And that involves some hard questions. If one of your rules is that your child must make his bed every morning before he leaves for school, and you find yourself nagging and arguing over it every morning, you have to ask yourself if this is a rule that is really important, and if it teaches real responsibility. There is nothing wrong with expecting children to share in chores. But it must be meaningful to them as well. One father in my workshop summed it up well when he said, "If you're not selective, you're not effective."

Question the shoulds. Are you doing something out of rigidity, or because your parents did it, or because your parents didn't do it? Are you doing something because that's the way your friends do it or because your favorite "experts" say to do it that way? Be careful about following advice that is offered as a cure-all. No system is right for everyone. Often, the simple question "Will this matter a week from now?" is helpful. Is it worth getting into a fight about spaghetti for breakfast or jeans with torn knees?

Setting rules is a confusing process for many parents, because they aren't sure what are appropriate limits to set. Every family needs some rules, but there has to be an understanding of which of these are negotiable and which are not.

One way of diminishing daily battles is to decide what is and what is not negotiable. Here's a typical dialogue that I hear repeated almost daily in my workshops with parents.

MOM: Janie, eat your string beans.

JANIE: I'm not hungry.

MOM: Come on, Janie, let's not start. Just have a few bites.

JANIE: I hate string beans. Why do I have to eat them?

MOM: They're good for you. Come on, just have a few bites.

JANIE (using her fork to spread the beans all over the plate): I'm full.

MOM: Young lady, I'm sick of these scenes. No wonder you're so skinny. You're going to sit there until you eat at least some of those beans. No dessert until you do.

Janie sulks, still not eating. Mom gets furious, frustrated by this endlessly repeated scenario.

Is this battle necessary? Is something terrible going to happen if Janie doesn't eat her string beans? Trying to get Janie to eat by telling her she's skinny is bound to backfire—and it's an attack on her self-esteem. Telling Janie beans are good for her will certainly not make her more eager to eat them. And many of us who were forced to finish our vegetables because children were starving in other countries would have been thrilled to ship our spinach and broccoli to these needy people by parcel post.

But when parents allow children choices and take their eating preferences seriously, they treat them with respect. You have to ask yourself: Do you really want your child to use food as a way to please you or to make you angry? And how much sense does it make to use dessert as a reward for eating beans?

What could Mom say instead? Perhaps she could respond to Janie's statement "I'm not hungry" by saying "Janie, only *you* know how your stomach feels. You can decide when you've had enough."

One less daily battle. Pleasant mealtimes. More autonomy for Janie!

I ask my students to draw up two lists, one of nonnegotiable rules, and the other of more flexible rules. They usually have a hard time with this. "Shouldn't all rules be nonnegotiable?" asked one parent. "If my kids know I'm willing to bend, they'll take advantage of it." On the contrary, by letting your kids know that some rules are negotiable, they're more inclined to be cooperative about the ones that are not up for discussion. It's a fact of life: A little freedom goes a long way toward fostering responsibility. Here's an example of one parent's lists:

Nonnegotiable Rules
1. Bedtime at 9:30 on school nights
2. No lying
3. No swear words in my presence
4. No name calling
5. Teeth brushed twice a day
6. No hitting or pushing
7. No throwing food at the table
8. No spitting

Negotiable Rules
1. Bedtime on weekends is flexible
2. Sometimes reading is allowed at the table
3. Piano practice can be skipped sometimes
4. Length of TV time depends on the day, homework, etc.

The mother of a teenage boy presented these lists:

Nonnegotiable Rules
1. No food in the bedroom
2. 11:00 P.M. curfew on school nights
3. Help with the weekly grocery shopping
4. No lying

Negotiable Rules
1. Cleaning your room daily
2. Talking on the telephone
3. Eating three meals a day

Parents often have trouble with this system because they fear it makes them look weak. But it's a fact of life that not all rules carry equal weight. There are always gray areas, and when you're ambivalent, it will be hard to enforce rules in any case. Children can sense when we say no and mean maybe.

8. RESTORE GOOD FEELINGS

I asked parents in my survey to describe how they went about making peace in the aftermath of an explosive confrontation. As we have shown, it's inevitable that we'll "lose it" sometimes, but that doesn't have to be the end of the world. We still have the option of talking it over or admitting if we were wrong or unfair.

Parents who responded to my survey were pretty unanimous in answer to the question "What do you do to restore good feelings?" in the aftermath of a conflict:

I say something like "Okay, let's look at what happened. I am very tired [usually true!]. I want to be sure I understand what's going on here." Sometimes it works, and sometimes I do this too soon and tempers flare again. I need to learn to let things *be* a little more.

I always tell my children I'm sorry I yelled at them, and sorry that I get so angry sometimes. I tell them I don't want to keep doing that, and maybe if I try not to yell, they can too.

I hug them and tell them I love them, even though I get angry at them.

After my young daughter and I have had a blow-up, we usually make up later by reading a story together. This is her favorite cool-down activity.

I get down on his level. Tell him why his behavior made me angry, and that I still love him. I hug him if he is upset or crying. Then I stay in close physical proximity to him until we're both back on track.

Generally, I apologize for losing my temper. I try to explain what made me so angry. I often talk about my feelings, and I try to get my children to share theirs. We always hug and kiss, and I tell them how much I love them.

We talk about it calmly, and then I ask them if they have any suggestions. Usually they do, and we discuss them. By then, we have all become friends again.

I always feel guilty. Usually, we apologize and then we discuss what has happened and make plans for the next time we get into a similar situation. Also, I try to tell them that I'm human too. Sometimes I had a bad day, I'm tired, or just don't feel like doing something—just like them.

Parents and children want and need good feelings to prevail, even when the battles become fierce. Time and distance heal many wounds, and a simple apology can diminish resentment and pave the way for reconciliation. Some people are afraid to let their children see that they are vulnerable. But it is a good lesson for children to learn. We are all weak sometimes. And we all have regrets. When we put a human face on the job of parenting, and acknowledge our imperfections, it makes it easier for good feelings to be restored.

If there has been an angry confrontation—and living in a family means that there will inevitably be conflict—it's important to restore good feelings as soon as possible—once everyone has calmed down. How this is done depends on the child and on the situation. Sometimes a hug and a simple statement like "Mommy loves you" does the job. Other times, especially with older children, a longer conversation is required—especially if a decision has to be made about a serious issue.

What about apologizing? Many people in my workshops report that their parents never apologized to them nor did they ever admit they were wrong. I think some parents worry that such admissions take away their authority. But it's important for parents to show respect for their children's feelings by apologizing when they say or do something they regret. By doing so, they also teach their children that everyone can be wrong sometimes, and that it's okay to admit it. There are many ways to say "I'm sorry":

Mommy shouldn't have shouted at you. I didn't mean to hurt your feelings.

I wasn't listening to the point you were trying to make, because I got angry when I saw the failing grade. Let's start over.

We had a hard time today, didn't we? What can I do to make you feel better?

I wish I could erase what I just said. I really lost it.

You must have been scared by my reaction. Let's talk about what happened and what else we can do.

I was wrong.

I'm sorry I lost my temper. Let's make up.

These eight techniques are not suggested as infallible formulas for handling parental anger. They are merely options that sometimes help to break an angry stalemate or encourage cooperation. And they don't always work every time. But parents are empowered by the realization that their "bag of tricks" is not empty, and that there are things they can try—solutions that have worked for others that can work for them, too.

10

The Loving Breakthrough

Our children give us the opportunity to become the parents we always wish we had.   —a parent

I stood in front of a group of about two hundred people who had gathered to hear me speak on the topic of parents and anger. There wasn't much levity in the room. I imagined that people who would venture out on a rainy night to such a lecture would be intent on learning something important. I wondered suddenly if I was up to the task. I began to speak, pulling out all my favorite stories, hoping to lift the mood in the room. It took all my skill, every funny story I could think of, to bring forth a weak laugh from the crowd at last. I wanted to stop and shout at them, "Hey, it's not so serious!"

Parenting *is* serious business, but often we take it too seriously. We can get so wrapped up in the weight of our responsibilities that we leave no room for the fun, the playfulness, the *joy* of being with our children. We may lose the ability to delight in their qualities of wonder, spontaneity, and silliness. Parents who attend my workshops and lectures care deeply about being good parents. But these

208

men and women are very hard on themselves—often too hard.

A father once told me how he spent a great deal of time working with his three-year-old daughter, teaching her about numbers and colors and the alphabet. But, he complained, "She is very resistant to my teaching her things. Like the other day, I was trying to show her how to distinguish different colors, and she got mad and wouldn't listen. I just don't understand it."

Parents need to enjoy their kids, rather than feel that they *always* have to be teaching them something, pushing them to learn, striving to advance their intellectual development and social skills. Children may rebel against these earnest efforts to educate them—they experience it as *pressure*.

The intensity of our concern and our earnestness can make parenting a heavy chore. It can harden our hearts so that we feel annoyed more often than we feel loving. It can cloud our vision so that we no longer marvel at these small human beings who have such a delightful ability to live in the moment, so much curiosity and energy. The light goes out, and we plod along, hoping to get from one day to the next without calamity, but failing to enjoy the process.

Finding the Good

"My name is Jean. I am a divorced parent with a thirteen-year-old daughter, Serena." The pretty, soft-spoken blond woman introduced herself to one of my workshop groups and, as I had requested, said a few words about why she was taking the class. "Serena has always been a sensitive, responsive child, but during this last year, everything has changed." Jean smiled weakly. "I know she's entering her teen years, but I feel that the changes in Serena's behavior have been extreme. We used to have a back-and-forth exchange. Now, there's nothing. As soon as I ask even the most innocuous question, like 'How was your day?' she turns off, says a curt 'Okay,' or shrugs, and that's the end of the conversation. She gives me the feeling that I'm intruding just by being alive.

"Things have grown gradually worse. A few weeks ago, Serena returned from summer camp, and now I find myself living with an obnoxious, rude, resentful child. I'm here because I'm hoping someone will tell me what I'm doing wrong, or how I can do better. Right now, our mother-daughter relationship is definitely not working, and basically I want to know two things. How to keep myself from killing her—and how to learn to be a more understanding and loving parent during the terrible teens."

A couple of Jean's classmates, themselves parents of teenagers, laughed appreciatively. But I noticed that another woman, who had described her daily battles with the "terrible twos" was fighting to conceal her horror.

"Yes, Patricia, it's true," I addressed her. "It may sound like a reenactment of the terrible twos. But I think the best advice is that parenting is something you have to take one day at a time." I turned to Jean. "What do you do when Serena ignores you or is rude?"

"It seems like I start every day determined not to let Serena get to me—to try to deal with her in some other way than by losing my temper or nagging. But usually she manages to get to me. I'll walk into the bathroom after she's taken a shower, and I'll just snap because there will be wet towels on the floor and soap melting in the bathtub and shampoo bottles left open. So I'll think, not only does this girl behave badly, she's also determined to turn our home into a pigsty. And I'll often just blow up."

Almost all parents go through periods in their children's lives—whether it's the terrible twos or the trying teens—when they want to ship them back for a better model. Or they fantasize about discovering that the hospital, where their child was born, accidentally switched him or her with someone else's baby, and they find that their true child is a responsible, polite, cooperative young man or woman. Most of us have said or heard other couples say: "He doesn't take after *my* side of the family." "Well, he certainly doesn't take after *my* side, either." Teenagers can be especially difficult because these once charming, cuddly children would now sooner walk barefoot over hot coals than speak a civil word to their parents. And it seems that the more you nag and yell, the worse it gets. You must set some limits, but it'll save your sanity if you don't sweat the small stuff.

"It wouldn't bother me so much if my daughter didn't treat me as though I were her butler and doormat," said Jean. "She never thanks me when I do things for her or says anything nice to me at all."

Dr. Haim Ginott once said that the tragedy of parenthood is that we are our children's friends and they don't know it—and they are not our friends and we don't know it. It's hard not to react in kind when our children turn on us as though we were their greatest enemy. We expect love or at least appreciation, and what we get is defiance, sullenness, and anger, which is bound to trigger our anger in return.

But let's face it. As parents, our primary role is to be the party poopers of our children's lives. We are the ones who have to say no, who must set limits, who cut short their fun. And this is why it's so hard for them to be grateful. Jean is the one who tells her daughter to do her homework when she wants to talk on the phone or tells her she has to be home by eleven when all her friends (or so she says) get to stay out until midnight. Yet, Jean expects her daughter to be grateful, and feels devastated when she resents her mother for doing her best. The tension increases as kids grow older, because, as emerging adults, they are constantly butting up against the necessary limits that we set. I've rarely heard a parent of a teenager who didn't voice a tale of woe like Jean's. But sometimes we get so bogged down in the negatives that we fail to see any good at all—this can happen no matter what age our children are.

I suggested to Jean that she try an exercise that many people find helpful. I call it the "Bug/Brag List." I asked her to take a sheet of paper and on one side write "Things That Bug Me About Serena." Then, on the other side, to write "Things I Appreciate About Serena." I thought she might be surprised at the outcome.

The following week, Jean arrived at the workshop saying that she felt much more positive about Serena. "The Bug/Brag List really helped," she said. "I went home and began. I wrote 'Things That Bug Me About Serena.' The list was easy. She drops her towel on the bathroom floor, leaves her sneakers in the hallway, her coat on the living room floor, and her school bag in the kitchen. She plays music too loud and wears jeans with big holes in the knees. She never tells me anything about her day. She barely speaks to me at all.

"Then I turned my paper over and wrote out a new list, 'Things I Appreciate About Serena.' What I listed was that she does her homework without any reminders, she doesn't complain about our not having very much money to spend, she always calls to let me know where she is. And she has a good heart. She helped organize a fund-raiser at school to feed the homeless during the holidays."

"Those are very interesting lists," I said. "What conclusion did you reach after you had done the exercise?"

"I looked down at my two lists for a while, and suddenly I realized that the things that bugged me were all pretty superficial," Jean admitted. "I noticed that the Bug list was dominated by things that had to do with messiness and her recent need for increased privacy. But the other list included things that were really substantial—that reflected her goodness and values. I decided that I could live with her not confiding in me—it was natural. On the whole, she was doing fine. I walked over to Serena and told her about my assignment and shared my findings. When I read the 'Things I Appreciate,' I said, 'Serena, I see that you are handling your life—you're dealing with all the important stuff real well. I guess the towel on the floor is not important to you. It *is* important to me, so tonight I will pick up the towel.' I put my arms around her, and we just hugged each other."

Similar breakthroughs happen all the time for parents in my workshops, even when they feel like they are at their wits' end. Techniques like the Bug/Brag List help them place things in perspective—something that is often hard to do during angry moments. Another mother, who did a Bug/Brag List for her two-year-old daughter, was heartened by the experience. Her Bug list included these items:

Screeches in a high-pitched voice
Won't play by herself
Won't take a nap
Disturbs me when I'm busy or on the phone
Won't share
Acts up in public and with my in-laws
Can't sit still for five minutes

Won't do what I ask
Won't leave me alone, especially when I'm tired

Her Brag list included the following:

Sweet, loving, cuddly, and affectionate
Bright and very verbal
Well-coordinated, self-directed
Enthusiastic
Persevering
Pretty good eater and sleeper
Tries new things
Loves to play with other children
Gentle with the cat
Sunny disposition

"She really has such sweetness!" this mother exclaimed with a glowing smile. "But it's so easy to forget sometimes."

It helps, too, as an ongoing effort, to look for ways you can praise your children for the things they do well. Sometimes kids feel that their parents only point out what they do wrong and constantly harp on the negatives. I give parents in my workshop an exercise in which I ask them to find several occasions during the week when they can praise their children in specific descriptive sentences that focus only on the positive. These are some examples from several parents:

I notice how skillfully your commas are placed in these
  math problems.
Kids, that was a very pleasant dinner. I didn't hear even
  a single little burp.
After her daughter dialed by herself and got a friend on

the phone: Those are the kind of secretarial skills I
could use in my office!
You spent a whole hour with me in the exercise class.
That takes perseverance and a lot of energy.
Grandma was so touched by your thank-you note. That
took time and effort.
What an intricate building! All by yourself, and you're
only six years old.

Evelyn, a teacher, related how she looked for ways to
praise the children in her class—taking the time to put her
words in writing:

Congratulations, Marshall, for completing all the inde-
pendent work quietly and on your own.
You're special, Jackie. You showed responsibility in caring for the class hamster without being reminded.
Good job, Maria! I noticed how you helped Norman,
our new student, on his first day at school.

"The notes help to target a child's efforts and give him
or her an incentive to improve," she noted. "The children
always keep their notes—they're very proud of them."
In *Parenting for the Nineties*, Philip Osborne suggests that
parents be conscious not only of giving praise but also of
lending encouragement. " 'You got an A! That's great!' is
praise, but 'You worked hard for that A, didn't you?' is
encouragement. 'What a good job you did!' and 'I'm so
proud of you!' are praise, but 'I can see you're proud of it'
is encouragement. The goal of encouraging remarks like
these," Osborne says, "is to recognize the child's effort,
contribution, and feelings of confidence and satisfaction,
and to avoid evaluative praise." In this way, we can view
our positive words as more than just "empty praise." Instead,

they become the foundation for our children to grow and change.

Give Yourself a Break

But sometimes it's not our children who disappoint us. Burdened by guilt and frustration, parents often confide in me that their true disappointment lies with themselves. They are convinced that they are not "good enough" parents, and that their failures are so overwhelming they cannot be resolved. Caring, committed parents in my groups make such statements as "I don't know how to be a parent." Or as one mother agonized, "After three years, is it too late to erase all the rotten things I've done and said?" I try to ease the guilt these parents feel by having them do a variation on the Bug/Brag List—this time, directed at themselves. At the beginning of the workshop, I ask them to think about their own parents. "What did your parents do that you try to emulate?" We list their responses on the board:

They rarely raised their voices.
They never insulted me or attacked my self-esteem.
They stood by me no matter what.
They never hit me.
They gave me a good sense of family.
They read to us every night.
They made each child feel special.

"Now," I say, "what things did your parents do that you try *not* to emulate with your children?" I write down responses such as these:

They were authoritarian, bossy, and rigid.
They never allowed us to express anger.
They weren't very affectionate.
They played favorites and compared us.
No matter what I did, it was never good enough.
They were inconsistent.
They didn't have a sense of humor—they were so stern and serious.
They would hit us for the least little thing.
They never apologized—no matter how wrong or unfair they were.

We talk for a while about their memories of their parents. "It helps to put your own parenting in perspective," I tell them. "Now let's talk about you. First let's list the things you would like to change about your parenting. Then let's talk about what you like about yourselves as parents."

The first list is always easy to create—the answers come fast and furiously:

I'd be more easygoing.
I'd never yell or call them names.
I'd learn to enjoy playing with my kids.
I'd be a better listener.
I wouldn't judge them so harshly.
I would smile and hug them more often.
I would find clever ways to handle the daily chores.
I'd read them two stories instead of one.
I would never spank them.
I wouldn't nag.
I wouldn't lose my temper so often.

The second list is always harder to come by. Parents aren't used to thinking of the things they do well. They're their own greatest critics. But gradually we get a few things up on the board:

I believe I'm teaching them good values.
I'm patient when they ask for explanations.
I can be silly with them, and we have fun together.
I help with schoolwork.
I mostly accept them and let them be who they are.
I say "I love you" every day.
I give them lots of hugs.
I am proud of them and really enjoy them.

Looking at the two lists, I tell them that this is what being a parent—or for that matter being human—means, that there will always be things we would change, but there are good things, too. You don't remember your parents as being all bad. Give yourselves the same credit for the ways you are loving, committed parents.

When I gave this assignment to Faith, the mother of a five-year-old boy and a two-year-old girl, it made a big difference. Faith had often expressed worry that she was handling her children all wrong. She was so hard on herself. Every time she failed to address a situation in the "right" way, she mentally put a check in her "bad mother" column. "I'm afraid the bad mother is winning," she told me one morning in class. "Every time I leave your workshop, I am determined to be better, but I always end up slipping. Something happens, and my good intentions fly right out the window." I gave her the exercise to do that week, and asked her to report the results at the next class.

Faith came to class the following week, looking a little less frazzled. "What happened when you did the exercise?" I asked.

She blushed. "Well, I guess I'm not *so* bad. But I'm not perfect, either."

I asked Faith to tell the workshop what happened.

"Well," Faith said, "I, of course, started out with the negatives. I wrote 'What I Would Change About Myself as a Parent,' and it was a long list." She read from a sheet of paper:

I wouldn't raise my voice so much.

I'd have more patience.

I wouldn't resent my children when they intrude on my peace.

I wouldn't try to force them to do things they don't want to do.

I'd try to be more interested when they tell me the excruciatingly long details about their superheroes or car collections.

I wouldn't say no as much.

"Those are the negatives. It was harder to do the other part of the assignment—what I like about myself as a parent," she admitted. "After seeing the list of negatives, I felt pretty low. But I forced myself to come up with some things." She drew a deep breath. "Okay, here's what I wrote under 'What I Like About Myself as a Parent' ":

I tell them I love them several times a day.

I hug my children a lot.

I always praise them when they make things or draw pictures for me.

I try to prepare fun foods that are also healthy, so they'll enjoy meal times.

[With my older one] I listen to his side of the story before
    I pass judgment.
I love them very much.

Faith finished reading and shrugged. "There you
have it."

"Did you learn anything about yourself from doing this
exercise?" I asked. "Other than the fact that you're very
critical of yourself?"

"First of all, that I'm not all bad. In fact, I realized I do
many things every day that are good. I also realized that
my children, most of the time, like being around me, so I
couldn't be too much of an ogre. It seems like the negative
things happen when I'm especially tired. I showed my husband my lists, and he said it looked to him like what I
needed was a break from twenty-four-hours-a-day mother
duty."

Faith's husband had a good point, and if she's lucky, he'll
help her get the respite she needs. Parents don't give themselves enough breaks, emotionally and physically. It's hard
to be loving when you're exhausted. Faith's story demonstrates something we all need to hear. Don't be so hard on
yourselves! Learn to see the good, not only in your children
but in yourselves, too. I'm not saying that all your problems
will disappear, but we can all benefit from positive reinforcement.

Lightening Up

Martin Greenberg, M.D., an innovative researcher on the
subject of father-child bonding, tells in "Fathers: Falling in
Love with Your Newborn," in *Experts Advise Parents*, about
the day he discovered that parenting his eight-month-old
son did not always need to be such a deadly serious task.

The family was squeezed into their small, crowded Volkswagen, and they had been driving for more than four hours. When they pulled off the road for a break, Claudia, his wife, asked him to change Jonathan's diaper.

"Is it pee-pee or poo-poo?" Greenberg asked her.

"Pee-pee," she assured him.

Without further ado, I opened Jonathan's diaper on my lap, only to notice a small round brownish object zooming out from the diaper and rolling around as if it were a ball on a roulette wheel. I followed it as if hypnotized. It finally rolled to a stop, lodging itself against my favorite beige sweater. At first I was stunned and said nothing. Then when I caught my breath, I looked at my wife and shouted, "Claudia, you told me there were no poo-poos!" My wife, attempting to stifle her response, had her fist in her mouth. . . . The more she laughed, the angrier I became. Finally, glaring in rage and frustration, I started the car and headed down the road. "Dammit," I shouted. "It's not funny. That's my favorite sweater."

For the next thirty minutes, Greenberg grimly drove on, glaring and saying nothing. Then, suddenly, he was struck by the complete silliness of the situation, and he began laughing so hard that he had to pull off the road.

"Hon, you looked so funny with that poo-poo in your lap," Claudia said, and this caused him to laugh even harder.

"Jonathan, sensing something amusing going on, added his own laughs to the shared mirth," Greenberg recalled. "Although he didn't know why we were laughing, there was something in it that related to him that made him feel good. We all hugged as a family and I felt an intense closeness that enveloped all three of us."

There is perhaps no greater comedy than the job of parenting—as evidenced by the popularity of the program "America's Funniest Home Videos"—yet when we consider ourselves as parents, we often focus on the aggravating, stressful, and deadly serious aspects of the task. Laughter can serve as a healing breakthrough that allows us, for even a brief moment, to experience in a positive way the absurdity of life and the absolute hilarity of many of the situations we encounter.

There are also moments as parents, in the midst of a seemingly endless stream of whining, crying, and yelling, when we are struck with an instant of empathy, which becomes like a window opening to release our frustrations.

Lynn, in the midst of a trying dialogue with her five-year-old daughter, experienced such a moment that allowed her to reach out with love. This is her account:

I put out a pair of tights.
I hate these tights.
I pick out another pair and start to help her.
Don't help me.
I stop.
No, help me.
I resume helping.
Don't do that!
I get out shoes.
I hate those shoes.
I put on the shoes.
No, no! They're ugly. They make me look like a little girl and I want to look like a big girl.
All of a sudden, I stop reacting to her oppositional behavior and feel her unhappiness. I bend down and give her a hug. All the anger of the morning disappears. "You're beautiful," I whisper in her ear.

There are times when we need to step back and do just the opposite of what our child expects. This, admittedly, can be very difficult. But to be able to change the mood and respond rather than react is powerful. Perhaps your child is cranky at the end of the day, and he doesn't want to eat dinner, and you're tired too, and you just want to yell at him. He is expecting you to get angry. The last thing he expects is to be comforted. Is he a physical child? If so, take him on your lap and say "Oh, you had a rough day. I know you're tired. What can I do to help you?" And forget about dinner. So what if he doesn't eat at five? At seven-thirty he can have an apple. Don't get yourself into such a routine that you can't ask yourself "Hey, is this really so important?

The father of a two-year-old once described a moment when, in a fit of anger at his son's oppositional behavior, he shouted "Act your age!" He said, "When I heard these words, I started laughing hysterically. He *was* acting his age. I was the one who was not acting *my* age."

We're usually unaware of how often we rush young children—who have *no* sense of time except the immediate moment they're immersed in. Sometimes I ask parents of children ages two to five to note the number of times in a day that they say "Come on" or "hurry up," and they are surprised with the results because, as one mother admitted, "I don't even hear myself saying it. It's just automatic, as though my son's full name was 'Harry-hurry-up.' "

Muriel, a very intense, hardworking woman who was always busily juggling career and family, told my workshop group how her six-year-old daughter taught her a lesson in priorities. "I'm the kind of person who schedules every minute of my day," she said wryly. "Up at six, shower, dress, breakfast, kids up and off, catch the train, work-work-work, race home, fix dinner, et cetera . . . et cetera

. . . et cetera. Sometimes I think that my kids' entire impression of me is this thing whizzing past on the way to the next activity." She laughed, then said, "Actually, it isn't so funny. Usually, it's quite grim. I think they're going to write on my tombstone 'Not now, I'm busy.' But my daughter, Erica, seems to have taken it upon herself to teach me to stop and smell the roses. Last weekend, we were at our beach house, and of course I had lugged along a pile of paperwork from the office. On Saturday morning, Erica and I went down to the beach, she carrying a pail and shovel, and I carrying my notes for a report that was due Monday. It was a beautiful, sunny day, and the beach was nearly empty. Erica settled down a few feet away from me, and I buried myself in my work. After about fifteen minutes, she came over and said, 'Mom, let's build a sand castle.' I sighed and said, 'I'd love to, honey [not really true], but Mommy has to work.' She begged. 'Oh, please, just for a few minutes.' I relented and got up, telling her okay, I'd help her start it, then I had to work. We sat down in the wet sand and started packing the mud. After a while, Erica looked at me, and her face was glowing. She said, 'Isn't this fun, Mommy? You never have time for fun.' There was something in her face and voice that really got to me. I could suddenly see myself so clearly in her eyes—always busy, always rushing around. Was all my running really more important than spending this precious time with my daughter? I felt teary at the realization—it was really quite a moment of truth. I smiled at Erica and told her, 'You're right! Maybe I won't work today.' We built the biggest sand castle ever, and I felt a deep sense of gratitude toward this child who helped me give myself permission to just sit in the sand and play. She hasn't stopped talking about our sand castle all week."

Time for Love

I was deeply moved when Mallory described the sudden awareness that changed the way she saw her four-year-old son, Jeremy.

"There was so much to do all the time—we didn't share many good times. Each day there was the struggle to get Jeremy dressed and to preschool and myself to work. After work, there was picking up a tired, cranky child, going to the grocery store, feeding, bathing, and putting him to bed, and doing household chores. I didn't have time to appreciate Jeremy. I was tired and tense and I always seemed to be shouting orders: 'Hurry up . . . not now . . . stop it . . . don't.'

"One morning at breakfast, Jeremy was whiny and feverish, and I could see that he was too sick to go to school. This was the last straw. Now I'd have to miss a day of work. And I wasn't looking forward to being cooped up all day in the house with a crying, demanding child. I was angry. I could find no sympathy in my heart for him at all. I sat across from him at the breakfast table, staring at his runny nose and his teary eyes. And suddenly, it was as though an electric current shot through me. I *saw* him differently. His soft, sweet little face . . . his sad little mouth that could so easily break into a smile . . . his round, warm, sweet-smelling body. My whole being was filled with such love for him in that instant that all my resentment and anxiety and anger were pushed away. At that moment, I really saw Jeremy, not as a source of aggravation, but as the gift to my life that he was."

When she told this story in class, many parents in the room had tears in their eyes. It was as though a light had broken through in the room, and we saw again that parenting was more than an endless series of chores and un-resolved dilemmas. In that moment, all the anger left the room. I hoped that that evening, in these households, there would be many parents looking across the table at their children and experiencing a new sense of delight.

Appendix A
Recommended Reading

FOR PARENTS

Ames, Louise Bates, and Francis L. Ilg. *Your Two-Year-Old* and *Your Four-Year-Old*. New York: Delta, 1980.

Balaban, Nancy. *Learning to Say Goodbye: Starting School and Other Early Childhood Separations*. New York: New American Library, 1987.

Balter, Lawrence, with Anita Shreve. *Who's in Control? Dr. Balter's Guide to Discipline Without Combat*. New York: Poseidon Press, 1988.

Bank, Stephen, and Michael Kahn. *The Sibling Bond*. New York: Basic Books, 1982.

Bloom, Jill. *Help Me to Help My Child: A Sourcebook for Parents of Learning Disabled Children*. Boston: Little, Brown, 1990.

Briggs, Dorothy. *Your Child's Self-Esteem*. New York: Doubleday, 1970.

Comer, James P., and Alvin Poussaint. *Black Child Care: How to Bring Up a Healthy Black Child in America*. New York: Simon & Schuster, 1975.

Crary, Elizabeth. *Pick Up Your Socks*. Seattle: Parenting Press, 1990.

Davitz, Lois and Joel. *How to Live Almost Happily with a Teenager*. Minneapolis: Winston Press, 1982.

Dombro, Amy, and Leah Wallach. *The Ordinary Is Extraordinary: How Children Under Three Learn*. New York: Simon & Schuster, 1988.

Ekman, Paul. *Why Kids Lie*. New York: Scribners, 1989.

Faber, Adele, and Elaine Mazlish. *How to Talk So Kids Will Listen and Listen So Kids Will Talk*. New York: Rawson-Wade, 1980.

———. *Liberated Parents—Liberated Children*. New York: Grosset & Dunlap, 1974.

———. *Siblings Without Rivalry: How to Help Your Children Live Together So You Can Live Too*. New York: Avon, 1987.

Fraiberg, Selma. *The Magic Years*. New York: Scribners, 1959.

Francke, Linda B. *Growing Up Divorced*. New York: Linden Press, 1983.

Galinsky, Ellen and Judy David. *The Preschool Years*. New York: Times Books, 1988.

Gaylin, Willard. *The Rage Within: Anger in Modern Life*. New York: Simon & Schuster, 1984.

Ginott, Haim. *Between Parent and Child*. New York: Avon, 1971.

———. *Between Parent and Teenager*. New York: Avon, 1971.

Jones, Sandy. *Crying Babies, Sleepless Nights: How to Overcome Baby's Sleep Problems—and Get Some Sleep Yourself*. New York: Warner, 1983.

Kitzinger, Sheila. *The Crying Baby*. New York: Penguin, 1989.

Kurshan, Neil. *Raising Your Child to Be a Mensch* * (*Decent, Caring, Responsible Person). New York: Atheneum, 1987.

Lansky, Vicki. *Vicki Lansky's Divorce Book for Parents*. New York: New American Library, 1989.

Leach, Penelope. *Your Growing Child—From Babyhood Through Adolescence*. New York: Knopf, 1986.

Lerner, Harriet Goldhor. *The Dance of Anger*. New York: Harper & Row, 1985.

LeShan, Eda. *When Your Child Drives You Crazy*. New York: St. Martin's Press, 1985.

Miller, Alice. *For Your Own Good: Hidden Cruelty in Child-rearing and the Roots of Violence*. New York: Farrar, Straus & Giroux, 1983.

Miller, Karen. *Ages and Stages*. New York: Telshare, 1985.

Osborne, Philip. *Parenting for the Nineties*. Intercourse, Pa.: Good Books, 1989.

Osman, Betty. *Learning Disabilities: A Family Affair*. New York: Random House, 1979.

———. *No One to Play With: The Social Side of Learning Disabilities*. New York: Warner, 1980.

Paley, Vivian Gussin. *Bad Guys Don't Have Birthdays: Fantasy Play at Four*. Chicago: University of Chicago Press, 1988.

———. *Boys and Girls: Superheroes in the Doll Corner*. Chicago: University of Chicago Press, 1984.

Quindlen, Anna. *Living Out Loud*. New York: Random House, 1988.

Samalin, Nancy, with Martha M. Jablow. *Loving Your Child Is Not Enough: Positive Discipline That Works*. New York: Penguin, 1988.

Schiff, Eileen, ed. *Experts Advise Parents: A Guide to Raising Loving, Responsible Children*. New York: Delta, 1987.

Simons, Robin. *After the Tears: Parents Talk About Raising a Child with a Disability*. Denver: The Children's Museum of Denver, 1987.

Smith, C. W. *Uncle Dad*. New York: Berkley, 1989.

Smith, Sally L. *No Easy Answers: The Learning-Disabled Child at Home and at School*. New York: Bantam, 1981.

Strean, Herbert S., and Lucy Freeman. *Raising Cain*. New York: St. Martin's Press, 1988.

Tavris, Carol. *Anger, the Misunderstood Emotion*. New York: Touchstone, 1982.

Visher, John and Emily. *How to Win As a Stepfamily.* Chicago: Contemporary Books, 1982.

Weinhaus, Evelyn, and Karen Friedman. *Stop Struggling with Your Teen.* New York: Penguin, 1988.

FOR CHILDREN

Alexander, Martha. *Nobody Asked* Me *If I Wanted a Baby Sister.* New York: Dial Press, 1971 (preschool).

————. *When the New Baby Comes, I'm Moving Out.* New York: Dial Press, 1979 (preschool).

Balter, Lawrence. *What's the Matter with A.J.? Understanding Jealousy.* New York: Barron's, 1989 (preschool).

Banks, Ann. *When Your Parents Get a Divorce.* New York: Puffin, 1990 (school age and preteens).

Berenstain, Stan and Jan. *The Berenstain Bears Get into a Fight.* New York: Random House, 1982 (preschool).

Blume, Judy. *Are You There, God? It's Me, Margaret.* New York: Dell, 1974 (school age and preteens).

————. *It's Not the End of the World.* New York: Bradbury Press, 1972 (school age).

————. *Letters to Judy: What Kids Wish They Could Tell You.* New York: Pocket Books, 1986 (for preteens).

Cole, Joanna. *The New Baby at Your House.* New York: Morrow, 1985 (preschool).

Crary, Elizabeth. *My Name Is Not Dummy: A Children's Problem-Solving Book.* Seattle: Parenting Press, 1983 (preschool and early school age).

Gardner, Richard. *The Boys and Girls Book About Divorce.* New York: Bantam, 1971 (school age).

Goff, Beth. *Where Is Daddy? The Story of a Divorce.* Boston: Beacon Press, 1983 (preschool and early school age).

Hazen, Barbara Shook. *Even If I Did Something Awful.* New York: Atheneum, 1981 (preschool).

————. *If It Weren't for Benjamin I'd Always Get to Lick*

the Icing Spoon. New York: Human Sciences Press, 1979 (preschool).

————. *Why Couldn't I Be an Only Kid Like You, Wigger.* New York: Atheneum, 1975 (preschool).

Joose, Barbara M. *Dinah's Mad Bad Wishes.* New York: Harper & Row, 1989 (preschool).

Krementz, Jill. *How It Feels When Parents Divorce.* New York: Knopf, 1988 (school age and teens).

Laiken, Deidre and Alan Schneider. *Listen to Me, I'm Angry.* New York: Lothrop, 1980 (preteens and teens).

Lansky, Vicki. *A New Baby at Koko Bear's House.* New York: Bantam, 1987 (preschool).

Mayer, Mercer. *I Was So Mad.* New York: Golden Press, 1983 (preschool).

Preston, Edna Mitchell, *The Temper Tantrum Book.* New York: Puffin, 1976 (preschool).

Quinsey, Mary Beth. *Why Does That Man Have Such a Big Nose?* Seattle: Parenting Press, 1986 (preschool).

Oram, Hiawyn. *Angry Arthur.* New York: Dutton, 1989 (preschool).

Rogers, Fred. *The New Baby.* New York: Putnam, 1985 (preschool).

Scott, Sharon. *How to Say No and Keep Your Friends.* Amherst, Mass.: Human Resource Development Press, 1986 (preteens and teens).

————. *Too Smart for Trouble.* Amherst, Mass.: Human Resource Development Press, 1990 (school age).

Sendak, Maurice. *Where the Wild Things Are.* New York: Harper & Row, 1963 (preschool and early school age).

Vedral, Joyce. *My Parents Are Driving Me Crazy.* New York: Ballantine, 1986 (preteens and teens).

Viorst, Judith. *Alexander and the Terrible, Horrible, No-Good, Very Bad Day.* New York: Atheneum, 1972 (preschool).

————. *If I Were in Charge of the World and Other Worries.* New York: Atheneum, 1981 (for all ages).

————. *I'll Fix Anthony*. New York: Aladdin, 1988 (preschool).

Wells, Rosemary. *Noisy Nora*. New York: Dial, 1973 (preschool).

Zolotow, Charlotte. *Big Brother*. New York: Harper & Row, 1960 (preschool).

————. *The Quarreling Book*. New York: Harper & Row, 1963 (preschool).

In addition, the following books are excellent resources for selecting books for children.

Fassler, Joan. *Helping Children Cope: Mastering Stress Through Books and Stories*. New York: Free Press, 1978.

Oppenheim, Brenner and Boegehold. *Choosing Books for Kids*. New York: Ballantine, 1986.

Trelease, Jim. *The New Read-Aloud Handbook*, second revised edition. New York: Penguin, 1989.

Wilford, Sara. *Tough Topics*. Stamford, Conn.: Longmeadow Press, 1989.

Appendix B
Parent Survey: Anger

The following form represents the questions asked parents in the compilation of material for this book.

I would like to invite you to participate in important research for my upcoming book, *Love and Anger: The Parental Dilemma.*

The following brief questionnaire addresses some of the issues I will be looking at in the book. I am eager to collect as much data as possible from parents like you. Your answers will be valuable in helping me to focus on the specific concerns parents have about anger. Please answer as many questions as you can, using more paper if you wish to elaborate on your answers.

All information you supply will be held in the strictest confidence. Your signature at the end of the questionnaire indicates your agreement that I may use the substance of your remarks in the book. Certain details will be changed to maintain your anonymity.

If you are willing to be interviewed further for the book, please include your name, address, and phone number. Return this questionnaire to:

Nancy Samalin, M.S.
Director
Parent Guidance Workshops
180 Riverside Drive
New York, N.Y. 10024

1. Your children are:

   Sex   *Age*

   ____   ____

   ____   ____

   ____   ____

   ____   ____

   ____   ____

2. You are most likely to become angry with your children in the following circumstances (check all that apply):

   ____ When they won't do what you say.

   ____ When they whine or argue with you.

   ____ When they tune you out or ignore you.

   ____ When they embarrass you in public.

   ____ When they won't take responsibility for themselves or their things.

   ____ When they fight or bicker with one another.

   ____ When they answer back or defy you.

   ____ When they dawdle or act spacey.

_____ When they bug you when you're tired or stressed after a long day.

_____ Other (please elaborate):

3. Describe in your own words what gets you the most angry with your children, completing the following sentence: "It really makes me mad when . . ."

4. Can you think of a time recently when some behavior of your child's made you feel angry and out of control? Describe the experience, recalling as much of a conversation as you can, preferably in dialogue form.

   Example:
   You: "Did you finish your homework?"
   Child: "I'll finish it later."
   You: "I told you to finish it before you turned on the TV."
   Child: "But it's my favorite program."
   You: "Turn it off now."
   Child: "You're mean!"
   You: "That does it! There will be no more TV tonight."

5. Do you have any techniques that help you avoid escalating confrontations when you are starting to get enraged at your child?

6. In the aftermath of an explosive situation or conversation with your children, how do you go about making peace or resolving the issue?

Other comments:

Would you be willing to be interviewed further?

_____ Yes _____ No

Name _____

Address _____

City _____ State _____ Zip _____

Phone (   ) _____

Signature _____

Date _____

AUTHOR'S NOTE:

I am eager to hear from you, and welcome your comments, reactions, and suggestions. Let me know what works for you and what difficulties you may have encountered.

Should you wish to contact me for information about lectures, workshops, and speaking engagements, please write to Nancy Samalin, c/o Penguin USA, 375 Hudson St., New York, N.Y. 10014.

Index